eBAY

LetteRS to eBAY

Hilarious **Auctions**, Crazy **Emails**, and **Bongos** for Grandma

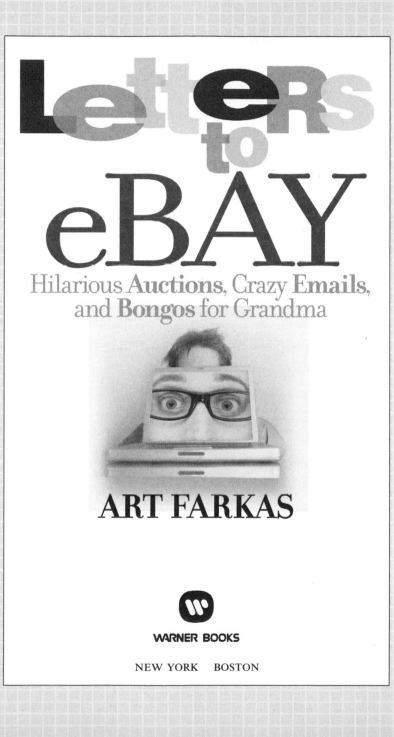

ART FARKAS

WARNER BOOKS

NEW YORK   BOSTON

Warner Books
Hachette Book Group USA
237 Park Avenue
New York, NY 10017

Visit our Web site at www.HachetteBookGroupUSA.com.

Printed in the United States of America

First Edition: August 2007
10 9 8 7 6 5 4 3 2 1

Warner Books and the "W" logo are trademarks of Time Warner Inc. or an affiliated company. Used under license by Hachette Book Group USA, which is not affiliated with Time Warner Inc.

Library of Congress Cataloging-in-Publication Data

Farkas, Art.
Letters to eBay : hilarious auctions, crazy emails, and bongos for grandma / Art Farkas.
— 1st ed.
p. cm
ISBN-13: 978-0-446-69958-7
ISBN-10: 0-446-69958-6
    1. eBay (Firm)—Humor. 2. American letters. I. Title.
    PN6231.E24F37 2007
    816'.608017—dc22

        2006101270

Book Design by HRoberts Design

Contents

Introduction

This book started because of Bunko. Yes, Bunko. If you're unfamiliar with Bunko it's the wildly popular dice game played by groups of women who scream uncontrollably at each roll in the hopes of rolling, well, a Bunko. Whatever that is. In my mind, these get-togethers are nothing more than a glorified tickle party. Anyway, if my wife hadn't left the house for her Bunko game this book would have never come to fruition. It all started one August night in 2005 when my wife scampered away to her cult-like group, leaving me to watch over our two small girls. As one who uses the world of media as a form of distraction, I had a few options over the next three hours. At that point in my life my brain was starting to melt from being subjected to over 10,000 hours of the kids musical group the Wiggles, so popping one of those mind-numbing videos in the VCR was clearly out of the question. The Web seemed a logical choice. With a child on each knee, I surfed the Internet for some interactive Web sites for my daughters to enjoy. After two minutes my eyes started to bleed from watching a computerized Elmo spin on his head. I had to click away before my manhood was totally stripped from me. Then an idea popped into my head. I had heard through the family grapevine that my brother-in-law had recently put a few of his wares to sell on one of the most popular Web sites in the world—eBay. As an eBay member myself, I decided to check them out. My life would never be the same from that moment forward.

After logging into my eBay account I found his items. Naturally, in the world of eBay, these dust-collecting items were hidden treasures ready to be gobbled up by an anxious and reclusive buyer in Iowa or an elderly shopaholic in Texas. These were the following nuggets of pure eBay gold he was selling: A pair of used size 13 Rockport shoes, a ceramic "The Last Supper" sculpture with Jesus and his disciples, and a set of country-style napkins with place mats and napkin holders. Inherently there was nothing too strange about those items. My brother-in-law simply wanted to get rid of some stuff and earn a couple of honest bucks. But what caught my fancy were the descriptions of said items. The description for his Jesus and Disciples sculpture stated "if you are a collector of religious artifacts then this is a must-have!" What? You mean to tell me that this Michelangelo meets Leonardo da Vinci sculpture is up for sale on eBay with the low starting bid of only 99 cents? Why hasn't it been donated to the Smithsonian, surrounded by a glass casing with those invisible laser security devices deterring would-be thieves? Wouldn't that be a more logical resting place for this obviously rare and collectable jewel? Indiana Jones surely would have searched the bowels of the Amazon jungle for such a find. There were so many questions that burned inside of me concerning this must-have religious relic, so I sent him a few over-the-top questions about this Last Supper sculpture. After firing off a few more outlandish questions about his other items he finally e-mailed me to say that I should do the same to other eBay sellers to see what kind of reaction I could get. And so it started. I trolled eBay and quickly found a lovely Copper Metal Flower Arranging Form Bird Cage that stated it was "Worry Free!" at the bottom of the description. Worry free? This didn't quite make sense to me so I decided to exploit it. How can a flower arranging bird-cage be "Worry Free!"? So I took on the persona of a character that suffers greatly from worrying about whether sippy cups are really safe, the GNP of Hungary, and the number 72. I asked if his Copper Metal Flower Arranging Form Bird Cage could really help cure my condition of worrying and help me become "Worry

Free!" like his description promised. To my delight I received
a reply the next day with the assessment that the "Worry Free!"
description was merely a reflection of the "ready-to-use nature
of the cage" and that it, sadly, would not cure my condition. It
worked. They bought it. If someone can take that question seriously then surely there would be more eBay sellers out there that
would think the same. Thus, my alter ego Art Farkas was created.

Over the course of the next ten months my obsessive-com-
pulsive tendencies were channeled in a new direction—firing
off-the-wall questions to unsuspecting eBay sellers about their
items. By day I was a simple fifth-grade teacher—by night I
transformed into Art Farkas. From the person selling a vintage
French bayonet to the one offering a ceramic bird feeder tray,
no one was safe from my onslaught of seemingly far-fetched,
creative letters. I was whooping it up pretty good, like a mad
scientist rubbing his hands together in mischievous glee. And so,
Letters to eBay was born. So sit back, put your hands around a
cup of piping hot cocoa and enjoy the Web mayhem that I created. And remember—these are actual auctions and responses
from actual eBay sellers. Oh, and by the way, the infamous Jesus
and Disciples religious artifact sculpture? It never sold . . . not
even for 99 cents.

New Large Copper Metal Flower Arranging Form Bird Cage

Decorative Bird Cage
Large
Directly Imported by Deals Only!

This elegant bird cage is a must for any
flower arranger/craftsperson!
Makes a wonderful "form" or frame
for arrangements of dried flowers!

The creative possibilities are endless!
Fits on any shelf or table!
Top Loading for easy cleaning/replacement of flowers!
Small front door with built-in latch!
Made of aluminum, which has been hand-painted
to look like weathered antique copper!
Painted aluminum looks elegant like antique copper,
but won't corrode or oxidize!
Perfect for outside arrangements, or for live flowers in pots!

Worry Free!
Dimensions:
13" in Diameter, 20" Tall

Hello and greetings! I am interested in your New Large Copper Metal Flower Arranging Form Bird Cage with the low opening bid of $14.99. Your description of said item has helped a lot in my pondering process. I have one thought though.

At the bottom of your description you say, "Worry free!" The simple fact is that my medical condition (please no inquiries in your reply e-mail) causes me to worry greatly about everything. I worry about simple and great things of the world including whether sippy cups are really safe, the GNP of Hungary, and the number 72. My question: Will your product really help me to be "Worry free!"? Believe me, I've tried everything to help fix my medical condition. (Again, NO questions please.) Thank you for your time.

Art

Hello-

Thank you for your interest in our auctions! The "worry free" line is more of a description of the ready-to-use nature of the cage. It is not a corrodible/rustable material and is ready to use right out of the box. It certainly does not extend to anything besides the cage. So no, this cage will not cure your condition.

Thank You,
Hunter at Dealsonlywebstore.com

Handmade Satin Organza Rose Flowers with Pouch-Doll-Quilt

Up for your consideration is a lot of 48 pieces of SATIN ROSES. These ROSES are a Pale Pink color and are SHADED here and there with a BEAUTIFUL SOFT Rose color. They have two SATIN PETALS and also 2 SHEER ORGANZA PETALS with a ROSETTE center and 5 SOFT GREEN leaves. These DARLING SATIN ROSES will come to you tucked in a sheer organza pouch embellished with a little flower on the front. This is a great way to keep these BEAUTIFUL satin flowers safe and protected.

The measurements are approx. 1½" to 1¾" round (the flower itself, not measuring the 5 leaves behind the flower).

Thank you for your interest in my auction.

HAPPY BIDDING from Pamela Amundson—the delight-fuldesigner

Greetings! Our daughter, Zoila, is set to attend her first high school prom in three weeks and my wife, Dotty, and I are making her dress. A very nice young man named Simon (freckles), who is president of the chess club and plays the french horn, is escorting her and we're pleased as punch! We held a three-hour interview with him last Monday and laid down the ground-rules for his date with our daughter. No monkey business and home by 9:00 is our policy. We have already purchased twelve yards of a periwinkle silk fabric, four bobbins of lavender thread, and a plethora of muti-colored buttons. We love your appliqués and think they would complement Zoila's new dress perfectly. But, as strict Presbyterians, we're concerned with the title of your auction. What do you mean by "Satin Organza"? Naturally, we're against Satin and his powers of evil and would not want to purchase anything having to do with Satin. If you could clear this up with us we might purchase your appliqués. Thank you.

Art

Good morning Art,

I awoke to check my e-mails and was also concerned with reading your e-mail. You sure had me questioning myself. I thought the spelling of Satan is with an a and not an i. So I got the dictionary out and wanted to make sure. Sure enough, this is the spelling of Satan not Satin. The description of Satin is a silky material that is glossy on one side. That is how the dictionary describes Satin. I surely would not include evil in my auctions. I have a Catholic background and was taught while growing up attending Catholic school that Satan was not the one to put my faith in. I would surely not include this name in my auctions, I can assure you. Have a great day and I was happy that your daughter has parents that are so wonderful to make her dress together. This will really make a lasting impression on her for the rest of her life. I am sure of that. It also would be a great honor to have made something to embellish her dress for her first prom.

Pamela
www.pamelaamundson.com

Large Lucien Legeard Trap
(animal trap, gin, rodent)

A splendid example of this large trap with a long chain and grapple hook 17" trap, 7" jaws, 44" chain.

It sets well, has a safety catch and is in excellent condition.

The maker's name Lucien Legeard is clearly stamped on the spring.

Five teeth are spaced around the jaws.

This size comes on the last row, which translates: for Jackals, Foxes, Otters, Wolves, Badgers. The use of Pole Traps was made illegal in 1904, similarly Gin Traps in 1958, but it is perfectly legal to collect these old antiques.

This will have to be my last set of traps for a while. I am away carp fishing in France early September, home for a few days and then off to Vancouver to return 2nd October.

I will then post more traps from my collection and who knows, I might even acquire some interesting ones during my travels.

Thanks to all my customers :)

Hello! I search eBay from 3:30–5:00 (after I feed the ducks) for interesting items. I have found something for my hobby here with your Lucien Legeard Trap. I belong to a group of men aged between 45–85 who enjoy the thrill of the hunt. We call our group "The Fugitives" and we hunt each other for sport. One person is chosen to be Dr. Richard Kimble and the rest are a part of Marshal Samuel Gerard's posse. It's just like the movie, where we give the person (usually it's eighty-two-year-old Glen) a head start, making him jump into a river or canal a la the 1993 movie. Then the rest of us hunt him down in the forest. He likes to hide in leaves. We can use any type of weapons, devices, and equipment we see fit to hunt our fugitive. I know that we would love to use your Large Lucien Legeard Trap. My questions: How long do you believe one could be stuck in the trap and still live? How much damage could it do to a human ankle? Thank you for your time.

Art

Actually the Lucien Legeard would be unsuitable. Firstly, the jaws are only 8" across and you would be lucky to get a man's foot in that small size. Secondly as it's a single spring, a human could reach down and release himself if caught. The British did have a man trap with double springs and plain jaws. But when these come up for auction they are terribly expensive because of their rarity. Cheers. Alan

Hobo the Clown Marionette—String Puppet

Hobo The Marionette

This string marionette is a clown dressed in bright colors. It's 15 inches tall without the strings.

As a child or a child at heart, this toy is lots of fun. Make Nellie run, dance, go to the floor and more. You can sing as he dances. Have Fun!

Accepted Payment : **PayPal**

This toy can make a great birthday, Christmas, Holiday present!

Hello! My older sister, Jane, is a big prankster and my brother Carlos (adopted) and I are planning to turn the tide. She once laid down 600 super balls on my bathroom floor and I broke my collarbone, ruptured my coccyx and sprained my right eyelid. You see, Jane is terrified of clowns ever since the state fair in 1988. She thinks they're "of the devil." My brother and I are planning on hiding 325 clown puppets around the church on her wedding day Jan. 12. We will place them in the balcony, in the pews (rows 3–12), near the candles, embedded in the flowers, peaking over the pastor's pocket, in her bathroom, in the best man's shoe, in the flower girl's bouquet, sitting on the piano bench, and manning the sound equipment. We also will hire four real clowns (The Mendoza Brothers) who will mingle with the guests after the ceremony. This will frighten her beyond belief! We can't wait! Will your Clown Puppet stand on its own or will we have to prop it up? Can it make any sounds? Thank you.

Art

Hi. The clown, as it is a marionette doesn't stand on its own and doesn't make sounds. It has strings. You have the control of its movement while playing with it.

The wedding day is a very special moment for the ones who are getting married—the parents, friends and relatives. I believe marriage is a terrifying decision on its own, when you think about the changes in your life that have to be made, responsibilities, economics and the possibility of having children to take care about. When you are at the altar getting ready for the ceremony, your whole life comes to mind, the good times and bad times. You re-evaluate life, before making the decision. I understand you want to make her payback all the terrible things she did, but she is your sister. It seems that even with all the terrible things that happened you still love each other. Think about it. At the end you and Carlos will always have in mind what happened at her wedding and its consequences. Maybe you can think of doing the clown thing in another activity with her. Sometimes there are activities before a wedding (rehearsal, dinner or brunch etc.). I know it's not my business, but I felt the need to write this. Take good care of yourself and your family. They are the most precious thing we have in life.

Thanks for visiting our store! The marionette is a good item to buy for someone to enjoy it. Maybe in time she will accept them, when she becomes a mother, you give it as a present to your nephew!

Take care,
Sandra

Meinl Headliner–Five Star Cherry Congas and Bongos

This auction is for a set of AA Meinl Headliner–Five Star Cherry/Chrome Congas and bongos with bongo stand. They were bought last winter and have been sitting in the corner of my room since. They are still in new condition for they have not been moved anywhere but to get them into my home. When purchased, the whole set was $460.

Greetings and hello! I was browsing eBay (I do so every day after *People's Court*) and stumbled across your auction. You see, my great grandmother Kiki has been living with my sister and I for nearly two years and she's driving us downright batty. She hardly does our laundry anymore too! We have decided it's time for her to go out and earn some rent money. We think that your Meinl Headliner–Five Star Cherry Congas and Bongos would be a great investment for us. We would set up the Congas and Bongos on the corner of 5th and Granite and Grandmother Kiki would drum to the walking public hoping for loose change. My questions: Do you think that the Congas and Bongos would be difficult for her to carry or would we need some sort of carrying device for easier transport? How much do they weigh? Do you think that she could play all four at the same time? Maybe the Congas with her hands and the Bongos with her feet? Thank you for your time.

Art

Hmmm . . . carrying them to the street corner. This task may be difficult but could be done. Put that conga stand around her neck, duct tape one to her back and one to her front and ride the bongos, with stand attached, like a horse. It would probably be better for transportation if you had a carrying device but can be done without. You may have to walk back a few times to grab the pieces you couldn't get before. I'm not sure of the exact weight but not too bad. All and all, I would say maybe 50ish pounds. If Kiki could play with her feet, then I would bet she could make a little money playing on the street corner.

Happy Birthday Hat Banner Banners Flag Flags

The Happy Birthday Hat Banner features a brightly colored birthday hat on a yellow background! The border of this decorative flag is done in multiple colors with stars, moons, flowers, birthday cake and a present! The word "Happy" appears at the top of the flag and the word "Birthday" appears at the bottom! This is a great flag to put out for everyone's birthday! This flag is brand new and in the manufacturer's packaging!

Greetings! I have a few questions about your Birthday Banner. I run a cock fighting ring and a very popular rooster named El Uno Con Grandes Talentos (The One With Large Talons) is celebrating his two-year birthday on February 18. It just so happens that he's scheduled to fight Mr. Bubbles that day (4–1 odds) and we wish to plan a party for him. His record currently sits at 28–4 and he has proved to be a most profitable bird for our business. As El Uno Con Grandes Talentos enters the ring, everyone in attendance will be wearing party hats, blowing those party horns, screaming, "Viva El Uno Con Grandes Talentos! Viva El Uno Con Grandes Talentos!" The spectators will be treated to one complementary piping hot churro. My wife, Conchita, and I are decorating the cock fighting ring. Could your Birthday Banner be attached to the barbed wire that surrounds the ring? Could we wrap El Uno Con Grandes Talentos in the banner, like a prize fighter donning the flag of his country? Thank you.

Art

Hi Art!

I have to say these are the MOST unusual questions I've ever had! The banner has a tube edge that would normally slip over a house flag pole or a vertical flag dowel. You could put a piece of twine or rope through this opening and tie it to the barbed wire pretty easily though, I would imagine. You could definitely wrap the rooster in the flag . . . it's a soft pliable fabric that would work well for this! Let me know if you have any additional questions and happy birthday & good luck to El Uno!

Billie www.blowininthewind.com

Vintage Sterling Charm
~ Large Heart Locket
~I Love You

This is a very old pretty that weighs 8.2 grams and measures 1¼" x 1¼". It opens up to heart shaped picture frames for a snapshot of you and your honey. Marked .925 inside. Sweet and sentimental.

Howdy! Your I Love You locket is exactly what I'm looking for. I am currently ranked #83 in the PBR (Professional Bull Riders) circuit but recently caught my girlfriend of four years, Shelby-Rae, cheating on me with a carrot top rodeo clown called Sprinkles. After I rode the bull, Mossy Oak Mudslinger, in Memphis last week, I proudly strutted back to my trailer for a cold one. It was behind Cody Lambert's trailer where I found Shelby-Rae and Sprinkles sucking face to no end. Sprinkles hadn't even the respect to change out of his barrelman outfit. There I was, staring at the love of my life crushing my heart to pieces. Shelby-Rae always said that she'd love me forever. Hogwash! I am going to confront Shelby-Rae. I will walk up to her and show her an I Love You locket and smash it to smithereens! That will show her! How solid is your locket? In your opinion, which tools would perform the most damage: crowbar, a sledgehammer, or pick-ax? Any suggestions?

Art

The locket would smash very nicely with a small sledgehammer. Please make sure that Shelby-Rae is well out of the way when you do this or you will be breaking rocks instead of hearts. I think we should collaborate on writing a song about this event. Perhaps a song entitled "Crushing My Heart With a Rodeo Clown." Maybe we could make a mint off of it, flaunt the money in front of Shelby-Rae and Sprinkles, ditch my retired rodeo husband (no kidding) and run away where rodeos and clowns don't exist. My husband says to tell you that there are plenty buckle of bunnies and Shelby-Rae ain't worth it. And by the way my husband knows Cody Lambert. Joe used to ride many, many years ago—in the Donny Gay era—and has the scars to prove it. Joe says if you see Lucky Lundegreen to tell him hello. Now from my point of view any woman that would fool around with a red headed man dressed up in a clown suit is not worthy of a hard old cowboy. So, buy the locket, smash the thing if it will make you feel better, and dump the trash.

Donna

P.S. Sometimes we watch the bull riding on TV. From now on when you climb on the back of that bull, imagine that you are riding Sprinkles and spur that sucker! And if you get thrown, like Shelby-Rae has thrown you, pick yourself up, dust your butt off and smile. There are a million girls watching you. You just gotta find the right one.

Drug Rep Sealed (40)
Notepad Lot Post-it Note Pad

You are bidding on a Drug Rep (40) Sealed Post-it Notepad Lot. This is Nice! From Monistat 1. Only the Doctors & Nurses get these! Made by Post-it! You will receive (1) Sealed Pack of (40) Post-it Notepads. Each measures 5" x 3". Nice Logos. Sorry for the bad picture.

Please e-mail us with any questions—Satisfaction Guaranteed

Your sticky notes could help me. Ever since I was struck on the head by an errant horseshoe thrown by my nephew, Kyle, I've been acting strangely and forgetting things. For example, last week I showed up to work (I own a day-old donut shop called Gobs o' Goo) with my collared shirt inside out and unmatched shoes on my feet. Saturday I got into a heated shouting match with the gas station attendant over the price of gas and threw a wrench at him. The final straw happened last night at the dinner table when I accidentally called my wife Hong-Yen, which was the name of my Vietnamese lover during my tour in Vietnam. I would use your sticky notes to help me remember things. I'm concerned, though, that your notes have the name of a drug called Monistat on it. I've been teaming up with Nancy Reagan since the 1980s and have said "NO!" to drugs. I can't, in good conscience, purchase notes that promote drug use. What exactly is Monistat? Is it a pill or does one smoke it? Thank you.

Art

Hi Art,

I'm in Las Vegas at the Wynn writing you on my laptop. Sorry to hear all of your misfortunes. Monistat 1 is a woman's health drug for a one-dose yeast infection medicine. It's made by Johnson & Johnson and might be an over-the-counter drug. I don't think Mrs. Reagan would mind this but I'm not sure. Go to Google and put in Monistat 1 and it will give you all the info. Thanks and good luck (especially the blunder with the wife). David

New Large Cat in the Hat Stuffed Animal

NEW LARGE (this guy stands almost 40" tall) CAT IN THE HAT cuddle pillow or stuffed animal. Your little Cat in the Hat lover will snuggle with this all day, it's adorable. 100% polyester, very soft. Ages 3+.

Greetings! Every year since 1990 my high school friends and I have performed a ritual on New Year's Eve. We douse a stuffed animal with gasoline, light it on fire and drag it behind a sport utility vehicle. It leaves a trail of burning debris on the road. Think *Back to the Future* meets Herbie the Love Bug! In 1993 we burned a 4-foot Bart Simpson. His face was melted like that guy from *Raiders of the Lost Ark.* In 1997 we stole my sister's vintage Barbie doll, shot bottle rockets at it, then dragged it behind a Ford Explorer for 3 miles. We felt like Thelma and Louise. Disaster did strike, though, in 2002 when James Berger (spectator) received 2nd degree burns on his ear lobe when a flaming, out of control Sponge Bob spanked him in the face. We need a new "sacrifice" for this year. Do you believe your Cat in the Hat would easily light on fire? When sprawling on the roadside, would its limbs (or hat) disintegrate or simply fall off? We almost caught a neighbor's junipers on fire last year. Thanks.

Art

Fires yet I have not set, no fires have I started.
And if this cat were to be lit, I'd just be brokenhearted.
But a sale's a sale and after all, he's really not alive,
So light him up if burn he must at twenty-four ninety-five.

6 Trays Individual Fake/False Eyelashes (Long)—#SGL03

You are looking on 6 trays long individual flare false eyelashes auction. It can be used for up to 36 pairs of eyes. It gives a Natural Look. Perfect for Brides or occasions where you still want to look natural. Our false eyelashes come from the same source with namebrand false eyelashes in the market.

Color: Black
Our Retail Price:
$1.99 per tray
Case Size: 4.25W x 2L x 0.5D inches
Length of Each Lash: 0.625 inch (1.6 cm)

Greetings! As a severe sufferer from EPD (Eyelash Pluck-ing Disease) I often find myself in awkward circumstances. My condition was supposedly cured by Dr. Winter but returned in 2004 while watching Clay Aiken sing on *American Idol*. When I was in fourth grade my parents sent me to a priest because I blinked uncontrollably. Now I pluck my eyelashes. Because of my compulsions I have my share of social issues. Just last week my date with Lisa Hartsell ended in disaster when I plucked 8 eyelashes and sprinkled them subconsciously into her piping hot bowl of vegetable soup. Also, I got fired from my job last Thursday. As you can see, I need a solution for my case of EPD. I could fasten your eyelashes and only pluck the fake ones, thus leaving my natural ones in mint condition and also deterring my compulsion! How many individual fake eyelashes per unit? 30? If I involuntarily pluck 7 eyelashes per minute, how long would each pair last? Thanks!

Art

Dear Art:

Thank you for contacting *FalseEyelashesStore.com*. We are sorry to hear your condition and we hope that our product can help you.

Answering your questions, each tray consists of 60 pieces of individual flare eyelashes. Giving us your scenar-io, we believe it will take 8.5 minutes for one tray consist-ing 60 pieces to last.

Please note, we carry three different lengths: short, medium and long. We currently only auction the long one on eBay.

Should you have any further questions, please do not hesitate to contact us again.

Red Cellophane Wrap 30" x 100'

This Is a Roll of Cellophane Wrap
Perfect for Gift Baskets, Floral Arrangements,
Gift Wrap and More!
Red
30" x 100', 250 sq. ft.

I am in the middle of putting together a play at our church. I penned the play myself. It's titled "Can't Touch This: The Untold Story of Shadrach, Meshach, and Abednego." The play revolves around the famous Biblical story of three Jewish men who were thrown into a fiery furnace by King Nebuchadnezzar and escaped unscathed by the flames. Unbeknownst to most historians, after they were promoted to the province of Babylon the three men opened up the first sauna and latkes business. Thus, SMA's Hot Rocks and Cakes was born. Anyway, we're having some trouble creating realistic looking flames and I was wondering if your red cellophane could do the trick. Our church pyrotechnics crew already burned a hole on the stage so they're fired. If we lit the bottom of your cellophane on fire, how fast would it burn? Would your cellophane resonate a red-like glow, like the real fiery furnace? This could give the audience a real sense of the heat and be quite a spectacle.

Art

Good Afternoon,

It truly is amazing what historians are uncovering these days. Hot Rocks & Cakes, who would have guessed? I wish I could give you a definitive answer on the cello, but I am really not sure how it would perform. I don't think it will burn, more likely it would just melt. You could bottom light it and that would work, but I don't know how hot your lights are, so wouldn't want to venture a guess as to how long before the flames became rivers of molten lava (that would be a different story wouldn't it?).

Good Luck with your production!

Cheryl
CreativeMerchandise

Large, Beautiful Happy Buddha Statue

Large, Beautiful Happy Buddha Statue [Good Condition] 12 in. x 12 in. x 7 in.

THIS IS A VERY OLD STATUE! IT WAS PASSED FROM MY GRANDMOTHER TO MY FATHER AND FINALLY TO ME! BUT I HAVE NO IDEA OF ITS ORIGINAL ORIGIN!!!

Hello! After ten years as a salesman in the fledgling accordion business I decided to become a teacher. My application was accepted by Our Lady of the Assumption and I was assigned fifth grade. My students come from the wealthiest of families who expect the finest education. For luck my students would rub a Buddha statue before taking my exams. Sadly, Jay Welty, a redhead, received a C minus on a quiz and smashed the Buddha to bits with a protractor and a glitter bottle. I am searching for a new class Buddha. I believe your Buddha would be a fine replacement but am concerned with the size of his upstairs equipment. I would have to construct a tiny brassiere to conceal his man-boobs. I don't need eleven-year-old boys snickering all day. How wide is his chest and back? Would a man made bra for a Buddha be considered disrespectful? Thank you.

Art

Art-

I believe that this Buddha would be a great replacement for the one that you lost! In regard to concealing his man boobs—that is entirely up to you and your discretion as a teacher. I do see your dilemma. However, personally, if I were in your situation, I do believe that eleven-year-old boys snickering would be unavoidable and giving Buddha a bra would only make the situation worse! Not to mention someone of this religious background may get offended. I would recommend leaving him uncovered or locating a small children's t-shirt to place over his head if you feel needs be.

However, once purchased, you may do as you please with your Buddha. His measurements are as follows:

- arm pit to arm pit = ~ 5½ inches
- elbow to elbow = ~ 11 inches
- across his back = ~ 11 inches
- total around him = ~ 26 inches

Thank you for your question and happy bidding!

Robert

LARGE CONCH SEA SHELL SEASHELL 6" FISH TANK AQUARIUM NR

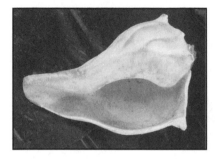

You are bidding on a beautiful CONCH SHELL, measuring 6" long. This baby weighs just under 8 oz. and is in perfect condition! I'm not sure where this was discovered, but it was on display in my uncle's home for nearly 10 years. Has no chips, nicks, dings, dents or other damage. Would look great in an aquarium or on display!

Please see my other auctions for more conch shells and other collectibles! I will gladly offer shipping discounts to those who buy more than 1. Thanks!

Greetings! My name is Art and I am a part of what I believe is the first and only conch shell barbershop quartet in America. We are called Conchelicious. We perform such favorites as "How Dry I Am" and "Workin' on the Railroad," but instead of singing those wonderful, feel-good harmonies, the four of us play the notes on conch shells. People love it! Last week we performed at the Garden Homes Assisted Living Center and they went absolutely nuts! There might have been a bra thrown our way, we're not quite sure what it was. It had lace. Anyway, the four of us each crafted our own conch shell to fit our part. I play first tenor conch, Sid Jacoby plays second tenor conch, Harry Poppen plays baritone conch and Tubby Pope plays bass conch. He has a really big conch. I'm looking for a backup conch in case my good one breaks. How big is the tip of your conch shell? My conches need to be small to blow higher notes. Do you believe your conch shell could play the part of first tenor? Thank you.

Art

Wow, that sounds amazing! I would love for this conch to help you out! Unfortunately, I don't know how to play it though. I've tried blowing into it, and nothing's coming out. I can hear the ocean when I put it to my ear, but nothing more. I don't see any cracks, but I'm not very musical, I'm afraid. The tip measures about .5 inches long. If this can help in any way, please buy it! That would be a fantastic story to tell my friends! Do you guys have a website or an album out? If you haven't already done so, you should consider doing a Christmas album or something along those lines—you could have a major hit on your hands! Or even do some Jimmy Buffet or Beach Boys' songs. It would be perfect! I've seriously never heard of anything like this, but I love it!!!! Please keep me updated!

—Dan

Hot Wheels WORLD RACE Highway 35
LOT OF 9 MOC NR

This is a Hot Wheels World Race, Highway 35
Lot of 9 cars.
Cars included are as follows:

#4/35—'55 Chevy Nomad–Wave Ripper
#14/35—Pontiac Firebird –Street Breed
#16/35—Zotic–Roadbeasts
#17/35—Twin Mill–Roadbeasts
#18/35—Moto-Crossed–Roadbeasts
#22/35—Krazy 8s–Dune Ratz
#24/35—Toyota RSC–Dune Ratz
#26/35—Sweet 16 II–Dune Ratz
#31/35—Red Baron–Scorchers

Every car is mint or near mint, case fresh
and comes with its own "token" and 12 page
comic.

Hello! I am attempting a rather unusual event for charity (Snickers Anonymous) and am looking to buy many Hot Wheels here on eBay. Ants and june bugs (net weight .0000053 OZ each) will ride on 325 Hot Wheels starting from Macy's and ending at Fujimiji's Japanese Kitchen in the mall. I have already secured rental of said insects. My cohorts (Pablo, Blair, Arnold, Rentie) and I will use an eye dropper to place the insects on the hood, inside the cars and in the trunks of the Hot Wheels. NO INSECTS WILL BE INJURED IN THIS EVENT! If one has fallen off his or her vehicle, caring hands protected by surgical gloves will pick it up. (We have practiced with lace wings.) Once they arrive safely at Fujimiji's Japanese Kitchen they will receive a nice treat — a big bowl of sticky rice. Local media has promised coverage as well as *Ranger Rick Magazine*! My questions: How big is the trunk space on your Hot Wheels? Do you believe each one could hold around 75 insects each? Thank you.

Art

Hello Art: First of all, let me say wow, your event sounds like something else! You do know how small these cars are, right? They are 1/64 scale, so they are only approx. 2 1/2 inches long. These small hot wheels do not have opening trunks, so I do not know how many bugs you could get into one as I'm not sure how you would get them into the trunk. This auction is for 9 different cars, and not all the cars even have trunks. How do you get such small june bugs? The june bugs we get here are large, and I couldn't imagine how to get more than 3 ON a Hot Wheels car, let alone IN a 1/64 car, but I'm sure you could get 75 ants into any Hot Wheels car that has open windows (not all have open windows). My suggestion for you would be to go to a store such as Wal-Mart, Target or Kmart where you can physically see & check out the various cars to determine which ones will work for your event. Good luck; sorry if I wasn't much help. Sue

NWT Midget Logger Suspenders 28" long Toddler Boys

Description:
NWT Midget Logger Suspenders 28" long Toddler Boys

These are also available in:
Sizes 24" & 28" with Grandpa's Helper, Dad's Logger or Midget Logger imprinted on them. See my eBay store to place an order for those.

IF YOU THINK THE SUSPENDERS ARE CUTE, TAKE A LOOK AT THEM WITH THE HICKERY SHIRTS. WE HAVE THESE AVAILABLE IN SIZES 6 mo to SIZE 10. THESE DO SHRINK SO I WOULD RECOMMEND ORDERING AT LEAST 1 SIZE BIGGER, IF NOT TWO.

Hello! I am gathering materials to create my prototype dolls. My doll line will basically follow the idea of Cabbage Patch Dolls but with a Pennsylvania Dutch twist. I call them Amish Dutch Kids and they will no doubt be a hit with kids. There's Rebecca, whose accessories include a lovely squared patterned quilt, pots and pans for kitchen duties and a butter churner. And Amos, who comes equipped with a goat milking stool, trousers and suspenders with easy to button straps, and a miniature black buggy with horse. As a bonus, Amos can transform into an adult Amishman named Josiah by attaching a Velcro beard (no mustache). Amish Dutch Kids will also be educational, as kids will learn about barn raising and the evils of electricity. Could I use your suspenders for the Amos prototype? Amos is two feet tall. Would they be able to stretch over his shoulders from just above his mid-section? I'm also tinkering with the idea of Mennonite action figures with kung-fu grip. Thank you.

Art

If the doll is 2ft tall I would think that the 24 inches would be best. Are you sure red ones would be best though? I admittedly don't know that much about the Dutch culture and attire but with Amish I know that a black pair would probably be better.

Best wishes with all that you do and thank you for asking. Please let me know if I can be of further assistance. What will these retail for? I have a children's store here and it might be a fun thing to include in my inventory! Thank you!

OFFICIAL HARLAND & WOLFF TITANIC CONSTRUCTION DOCUMENT

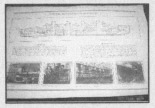

THIS IS A VERY RARE LIMITED EDITION REPRODUCTION COPY OF THE CONSTRUCTION DETAILS OF THE

R.M.S. TITANIC

Stamped by Harland & Wolff (builders of the Titanic) confirming it is an exact

Reproduction of the original plans

THESE CONSTRUCTION DETAILS WERE PRINTED SOME YEARS BACK EXCLUSIVELY FOR THE ULSTER TITANIC SOCIETY

WITH THE FULL COOPERATION AND HELP OF THE TITANIC SHIPBUILDERS HARLAND & WOLFF: QUEENS ISLAND: BELFAST AND ENDORSED BY THE ULSTER TITANIC SOCIETY LTD

The item is in excellent condition and measures approx 425mm x 295mm
The top half of the item shows a detailed sectional technical drawing provided by the shipbuilders Harland & Wolff.
Under the heading "construction" it shows the 16 watertight compartments separated by steel bulkheads with watertight doors between each section. It also describes how these doors could be closed by means of a powerful electric magnet controlled from the captain's cabin, or in the event of an electrical failure, by means of levers situated near the doors. The bulkheads fore & aft extended upwards from the keel to five decks above and amidships four decks up. It also mentions the White Star claim that any two compartments could be flooded without involving the safety of the vessel in any way! Also shown is the position of the engine rooms and boiler rooms.

Greetings! I belong to a group of middle-aged males who simply adore and worship the great movie *Titanic* starring Leonardo DiCaprio and Kate Winslet. We meet once a month and call ourselves "Hijos del Corazon del Oceano." English translation: Sons of the Heart of the Ocean. Our fellowship includes acting out our favorite classic *Titanic* moment (the painting scene has been banned), throwing darts at that horrible Billy Zane and cry sessions to Celine Dion's "My Heart Will Go On" by candlelight. Pepe (37, Gap employee) has even knitted us quality hats like the one Jack wore when he was looking for Rose on deck F. Every meeting we each bring a new piece of *Titanic* memorabilia to share. I've about exhausted all my resources and am searching eBay for new and exciting *Titanic* items. I absolutely love your *Titanic* Construction Document! Does it showcase the mistake that Harland and Wolff made on the manifold located below the exhaust port? People don't know about that. Thank you very much.

Art

Hi, Art. Nice to hear from you. From where I am sitting at my study window I can see the Harland & Wolff shipyard giant cranes Samson and Goliath towering over Belfast city. I can also look at Belfast Lough where the *Titanic* sailed out on its maiden voyage. On top of that my grandfather helped build the *Titanic* and I grew up listening to many fascinating stories about the great ship. I still have lots of his tools and other items. My grandfather always said that the sinking of the *Titanic* was a disaster—the building of the great ship was not! The Construction Document is an actual construction drawing reproduced by Harland & Wolff and would have been issued before the ship sank. Being a commercial company, they are not going to highlight any mistakes, are they? The Thomas Andrews Notebook that I have also up for auction shows details like this which may contain the fault you are looking for. If I can be of any further help, please get back to me.

Best wishes
Ernie

Bud Vase Message Center,
CHALKBOARD, CORKBOARD

Bud Vase Message Center

Stylish and practical, this wood message center with chalkboard, corkboard and chalk ledge also holds two glass tubes for showing off your favorite blooms. Includes chalk and eraser.
22½" h x 13" l x 1½" dp

Hello! What an incredible find here on eBay! I am a simple bricklayer and often come home from a hard day's labor tired and weary. My beautiful wife, Keri-Mae, offers to give me back, neck, and leg rubs but finds herself generally worn out after 2–3 minutes. This is very frustrating. I'm not sure why we've never seen a message center at Wal-Mart or Target before but we're very interested in yours. What is the best way to use your message center? Should I lay down with my back resting on the corkboard? That seems as though it would be uncom-fortable. Maybe I could lay my legs across the chalkboard, so Keri-Mae could have easier access to rub my calf muscles. We kind of don't know how it works. Also, should we lay your message center flat on the carpet or propped on the couch, for extra stability? I think that's what the professionals do. Thank you for answering my questions. Your Bud Vase message cen-ter could really help Keri-Mae message me better.

Art

Hi,

I am trying to figure out what you are asking me. As I re-read your question, I think you are thinking it reads as MASSAGE center, where it is a MESSAGE center, to write notes on. This isn't for body use, it is to hang on a wall.

I was in JC Penney last week and they have MASSAGE items there I think you would be happy with. Hope this helps and clears things up.

Kathy

Adorable Hello Kitty Plush Backpack Purse Bag

You are bidding on an adorable Hello Kitty Plush backpack bag/purse for that special child or collector. This is in excellent condition. It probably has been used but is in excellent condition. The material of kitty is soft and plush. Would make a great gift. From head to toe on bag is about 13 inches tall. Check out my other Hello Kitty items.

Hello! I am the only male on my high school J.V. cheer-leading squad. Naturally, I have received much ridicule for this choice (including an extremely rude algebra teacher). The girls have decided to wear Hello Kitty backpacks during homecoming week as a show of unity. Blair has chosen a pink one, Mercedes has a teal one and Uniqua will be sporting a baby blue one. I voted for My Little Pony apparel but was laughed at by the girls (they also put me at the bottom of the pyramid). We're playing St. Augustine for homecoming and they're the defending state champs! Our best player, Kyle Smith (6 feet tall and a bag of chips), is our only hope. We need all the luck we can get so I'm searching eBay for the best Hello Kitty backpack possible. Despite the possibility of more ridicule, I'm willing to don my backpack for the sake of the team. Do you believe the backpack could hold the following: three books, one binder, lip gloss and seven pencils? Thank you for your time.

Art

Hello. Thanks for your question. What a great story to tell. You are a brave man! I think that this bag in particular would only hold the lip gloss and seven pencils. I do have another Hello Kitty tote on eBay that, depending on size, could hold perhaps 2 books and the binder, but is not as fancy, maybe even a little plain. I hope that your quest for the perfect bag will be fulfilled. I wish you and your team much success. Good for you! More people should be like you. If I can be of further help please let me know. And once again, congrats and I wish you much success with your special quest! Kindest Regards,

Kadrmasfinds

Pro Portable Artist Easel Mega $300 Art Supplies NR

Compare at $300.00+

Artist's Studio Set
with a Beautiful Solid Wooden Sketchbox Easel!

This all wood teak-finished easel is adjustable & folding with attractive classic gold hardware. Works as either a floor easel or a tabletop easel. It's portable for the traveling/ outdoor artist with a shoulder strap and a handle. (No Assembly Required.) Also makes a great conversation piece for your den, office or living room.

One of the only FINISHED easels you'll see on eBay. Your local art store does NOT have this easel.

Hello! I am an oil painter but have an affliction that no doubt limits my potential for a lucrative career. My paintings have been compared to Pablo Picasso meets the genius of Bob Ross (happy trees) by many, including my mentor Dr. Sigfried Copenhagen. You see, I have been diagnosed with Trigeminal Droopocous in my left eye—or "The Lazy Eye" as it's more commonly called. Because of my affliction the left half of my paintings are usually a jumbled mess of awkward zigzags and poorly placed objects. In Jr. High I was placed in the 97th percentile of cock-eyedness. I hate it! I also have trouble crossing over with my right hand to reach over to the left side of the canvas. I'm interested in purchasing your easel and am wondering if the left leg could be lowered about eight inches to accommodate my lazy, droopy eye, with the right leg staying put. Could that cause the easel to tip over though? I believe that would help my paintings become more presentable and even. Other suggestions? Thank you.

Art

The legs are adjustable, but of course the canvas would be uneven. I know a neurologist and brain scientist who has got some good results using well placed mirrors in therapy for "phantom limb syndrome," in that case "tricking" the brain to make adjustments based on the image in the mirror. I wonder if there would be a way to place a mirror or mirrors that would allow you to use the other eye to paint the left side of the canvas? I'm not sure what I'm talking about here, because the image may be backwards, but just an idea. If you found the mirror to be helpful, you could always have a custom stand made to accommodate such a device. Thanks, David

NEW HANGING DRAGONFLY DESIGN CERAMIC BIRD FEEDER TRAY

This is a great yard style planter and/or bird feeder

This bird feeder/planter/candle holder is perfect for outdoor and patio design. It comes ready to hang and has a clever design to go with its functional capabilities. This piece is beautiful and would make a fine gift for a neighbor or close friend.

This bird feeder is 10" tall (standing) and the overhang hood measures 10" diameter.

Hello! Like most good-hearted country folk, my wife, Eunice, and I enjoy sitting on our porch at night, drinking piping hot cocoa in the winter or freshly squeezed lemonade in the summer. Eunice usually coaxes me to play a tune or two on my Hohner American Ace harmonica. She loves "Oh Susanna" and "She'll Be Coming Around the Mountain" and has been known to break out in a little jig every so often. (I've caught that dirty-bird Larry Buckhalter across the street with binoculars on more than one occasion.) We love watching birds grace our humble porch and are looking for a new bird feeder after a wayward broom handle broke our last one. We're looking for one that we could fill with alcohol. Eunice can sure make me laugh when she's a bit tipsy at weddings and we think that drunken birds would be an absolute hoot to watch! How fun would it be to see birds get crazy and nuts? Would your bird feeder be able to hold liquids or just solid food? Would they be able to put their tiny beaks in and drink the stuff? Thank you.

Art

We certainly don't recommend the bird feeders as objects to distribute alcohol to birds since there is no real age of consent established for birds. We would be remiss to recommend such a use without discernment. Could the tray support a shot or two of magic elixir? Sure it could. Beware though because such influences may send your birds into a crazed tizzy causing them to attempt to catch breezes that don't exist and to crash into windows and fly into open houses. While that might prove to be entertaining for Eunice's fun-loving spirit, it could prove a hazard as well, so we recommend caution and will leave the final decision to you.

And don't give ol Larry such a hard time. I'm sure Eunice is quite a treasure on the eyes and seeing her delight to the tune of your skilled mouth organ melodies is enough to conjure up the boyhood desires of even the most innocent of men.

Boys will be boys . . . should be no harm if he's only peeking.

Hope you find our bird feeder meets your needs, and if not, it was a pleasure to have you stop by.

Old Catcher's Mitt Bill Dickey Vintage

Old catcher's mitt for the left hand. It is embossed with Bill Dickey's signature. The glove is also stamped "Cowhide" and "Sporting Marathon Goods." It's in nice shape — no rips or tears in the leather. The leather lacing is complete. There is some nonvisible fraying of the wrist lining. The glove was apparently owned by a ball player named "Mike" who printed his name on the backside 3 times in ink. The ink has faded over the passing years. The dimensions of the glove are 11"X10".

Greetings! My wife and I are expecting our first child in December and can't be any more ecstatic! My wife, Norma, and I are well versed in the ways of early American settlers and love to play the part. We make butter from scratch, have no microwave (invented by Lucifer himself) and have chosen to have a natural birth. Believe it or not, I'm a former Junior College catcher and my love for the glove still abounds. My wife has agreed to a silly dream of mine. When little Willy is birthed I will be squatting near Norma's you-know-what with full catcher's garb on. Mask, chest protector, shin guards, and of course a cup complete with athletic supporter. I will signal for a fastball and BOOM! little Willy will squirt out into the world and into my glove. Somehow, my trusty catcher's glove has been misplaced. I am looking for a new one to purchase on eBay. Do you believe your fine catcher's mitt will be able to catch little Willy? Would it absorb all the "junk" that comes with him?

Art

    If little Willie doesn't throw you a curve, and assuming there is not too much spin, I believe the Bill Dickey Glove is up to the task! Your primary challenge will be to distinguish little Willie from that junk accompanying him.

5 Rolls of Colored Duct Tape, Pack, Mend, Repair, Tools

Here are five rolls of quality duct tape in four different colors. If you are tired of being teased about silver tape, this is the answer. It comes in tan, white, navy, and black and I will throw in a second of one of these colors; one (or more) of each color is included in this sale. It was made in the USA!

Each roll contains 10 yards of 2" tape for a total of 50 yards of sticky tape. This will fix almost anything that is broke—ha. And the best part is that it will match the decor.

Hello! I am a self-employed bumper sticker creator. Perhaps you've seen some of my creations plastered on car bumpers. I've come up with such popular catch phrases as "My Grandkids Barfed on Your Grandkids," "Happiness Is Kicking Your Dog" and "John Kerry: Why the Long Face?" Production costs have become too high as of late and an idea recently popped into my head. Why can't I simply purchase rolls and rolls of duct tape and write my critically acclaimed catch phrases on 10-inch strips of duct tape with a black pen? This would cut my supply costs by 87%. Imagine a customer proudly displaying his newly applied duct tape bumper sticker with the phrase "Save the Owls: Poach an Eagle Instead." I think this would not only be aesthetically pleasing to the eye but would be environmentally conscious as well. How long do you think your duct tape will stay stuck on a car bumper? When would the edges start to peel off? After two months? A year? Thank you.

Art

An interesting concept but don't most people associate duct tape to rednecks? Regardless, I am not sure how long they would last on bumpers. I have a hunch the tape would outlast the message. I lived in AZ for years and duct tape is a household thing; it held canopy windows in for 2–3 years before giving out. Now I am in WA and I think the rain would wash the tape clean in a short time. All I can recommend: TRY SOME. If it works, maybe we can make a deal on a mass quantity.

Lot 15 Bath & Body Works Hand Soaps All Scents!

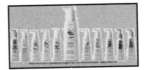

Up for bid is a huge lot of <u>15</u> brand-new never been used bottles of Bath & Body Works Moisturizing Hand Soap.

<u>*This is a $75.00 Value!*</u>

I have just about every scent, so I am allowing the winner to individualize this auction by choosing the scents he or she wants!
-OR- you could have fun and let me pick the scents!

Thank you, thank you! A quick story before my questions. My left hand was taken from me in a childhood accident when I was a mere nine years old. My older brother, Andrew, was conducting an experiment with a model airplane, a stick of butter and a chain saw (doomed to say the least). I have endured many obstacles in life and one of my only solaces is the warm feeling of bath water upon my stub. (I've nicknamed him Slappy.) You state in your description of your item that it is "hand" soap and not "hands" soap. Not too many companies specialize in items only made for "hand." Usually such items are made for people that have both hands. (I call them BHPs, I sometimes spit on them.) So, you can imagine my excitement when I came upon your item. My questions: Will Slappy be able to push down on the top to dispense or could it hurt him? Are the contents easy to replace, say, with goat's milk? Slappy loves goat's milk. I type pretty good with one hand, don't I? Thank you for your time.

Art

You have a great personality, and you type amazingly well for a person with only one hand! The contents of the bottles are easy to replace when empty, the top just unscrews. Also, I think it would be OK for Slappy to dispense, but I don't have any experience in that, nor do I know anyone with one hand, so I have no one to ask. They seem relatively easy to pump, and if you can pump other things, like lotion, etc., I don't think you would have a problem with it. Or you could just use your hand, no? Thank you for inquiry and have a wonderful day!

3m Jumbo Lint Roller!
20 pack of Lint Rollers!

3MJUMBO
LINT ROLLERS

ULTRA TACK ADHESIVE
Made with SCOTCH Brand Adhesive

* * * * * * * *
You are Bidding on 20 Lint Rollers!
* * * * * * * *

These are not just the refills.
<u>Each roll has its own handle.</u>

Each JUMBO roll is 4 inches wide and 39 feet long and has 70 sheets so they are 25% more than the traditional 3M roll only having 58 sheets. You get 20 of them!

The total length of your 20 rollers is 760 feet and have 1400 sheets that can be torn off to renew the ultra tacky surface for a renewed lint pickup.

These lint rollers are compact and great for using anywhere you go. They can be used at home to remove pet hair and lint from clothes or upholstery, even automobile upholstery. They are great when you are traveling.

Greetings! Your fabulous jumbo lint rollers could be a godsend for my family. You see, our pet porcupine, Maria, has a nasty hankerin' for shedding her quills all over our house. We legally adopted Maria after we found her shivering in an alley eating day-old maple bars. Despite her blunt-nosed face, long curved claws, and razor-sharp barbs, she has become a fine pet. Our nine-year-old daughter, Elva, has grown quite fond of Maria and recently knitted her a lovely country style sweater. Our vertically cross-eyed son, Jasper, often spoon-feeds her Lucky Charms cereal. In the past we have picked up her fallen quills with an old-fashioned "pooper-scooper." How durable and effective are your jumbo rollers? Maria often sheds 2-inch-long clumps on top of our NASCAR rug. Simply put, do you believe the ultra tack adhesive would be able to pick up a porcupine's quills or would they not stick at all? Thank you.

Art

Art,

I have spent hours reading over the 3M specification sheets for the lint rollers. Unfortunately, there is no mention of porcupine quills. The 3M Jumbo Lint Rollers do a terrific job picking up pine needles. Pine needles are long and have sharp ends, but being such a distant cousin of the porcupine quill is probably not a good reference point.

The major concern with using the Jumbo Rollers to pick up the quills is not the rollers' ability to do so, but the damage to the roller operator's hand while those sharp quills whip around the roller, slashing the user's hand.

Due to this potential hazard, it is not relevant if the roller will or will not pick up the quills. We simply do not have a large enough area on the roller to print the eighteen line (12 point font) warning label that would be necessary to endorse the cleanup of quills with this product.

By the way, our research shows that porcupines do not shed their quills, only their hair. The 3M Jumbo Lint Rollers will work great for that!

Lot of 60 Tennis Balls —great dog toys!!!!!!!!!!!!

Up for bid we have this box of slightly used tennis balls, mainly Wilson and Penn. These make the absolute greatest dog toys money can buy. They are also great for walker tips, furniture legs, kids' baseball or whatever else you can think of. This is a box of 60 tennis balls.

Hello! Starting on August 9 I am opening up a summer sports camp for kids aged 4–8 and have a few questions about your tennis balls. My camp is an answer to all of today's political correctness that shrouds our youth sports programs in darkness. They are a breeding ground for sissies. My camp teaches mental and physical toughness and what it takes to succeed not only on the athletic field but also in the game of life. Here are the four laws of my camp: 1. Only winners get ice cream. 2. We're only as good as our weakest player. 3. Always listen to the parents' yelling (parents ALWAYS know more than you). 4. Losing is for girls. Camp members will recite the laws three times a day. There's a game we play called "Death Ball" where we need balls that have a high bouncing range. How tight are your tennis balls? If they were launched from atop a 40-foot scaffold, how high would they bounce off pavement? How about off a small child? Thank you.

Art

Art,

I'm really proud of you for doing what you are doing for the youth in your area. As for your questions, How tight are your tennis balls? If they were launched from atop a 40-foot scaffold? How high would they bounce off pavement? How about off a small child? I have absolutely no way of answering these questions. I am 59 years old and I am not going to climb atop a 40-foot scaffold to see how high the balls bounce off pavement, as I am sure I wouldn't bounce at all when I fell. These are very simply used tennis balls. I bought too many for toys for my dogs and am trying to re-sell a lot of them at a loss. That's the best information I can give you. Is this a joke or what???

Lot of 5 Sets Rubber Stamps, All Occasion, Wedding, Etc

This is a lot of 5 sets of rubber stamps. All have been gently used. There is some ink on the front of the all occasion stamps, looks like my daughter scribbled a little. Takes nothing away from using or seeing the label of the stamp. There is a wedding set, can also be used for anniversary. There is another set of 4 stamps that has a beach theme, a Christmas theme, a butterfly theme, and a baby theme. There is a set that is one stamp 5x7 with a block border. There is a set of 4 stamps with a cute angel theme w/a scripture saying "thou hast put gladness in my heart," Psalms 4:7, and the last set contains 8 all occasion stamps which are as follows: 1) hello 2) best wishes 3) happy birthday 4) welcome baby 5) to someone special 6) miss you 7) thinking of you 8) thank you.

I forgot to mention that all stamps have initials on the side of them. A wonderful group of us get together and stamp and we found it was the only way to keep our stamps from getting confused.

Greetings! As an innovative fifth grade teacher who incorporates shame (an under-rated emotion) into his curriculum, I have a wonderful idea that would promote learning. Inspired by the book *The Scarlet Letter,* when a child performs poorly on a test, acts out in class or forgets their homework, I will brand them with a mark upon their forehead. I have chosen to use rubber stamps as my tool. For example, if Jack Falls (class bully) receives a 43% on a math test I will stamp the words "Math Failure" on his forehead for the entire school to see. Shame can be very effective with young children. The other students will shun the offender and therefore will cause him or her to study harder. Parents agree. I have written an article for submission on this subject to *Teaching Matters* magazine. How easy will your rubber stamps glide on a student's forehead? Will the ink fade away in 2 or 3 days? Do you have the word "Loser" on a rubber stamp? Thank you. Your stamps could help an entire generation learn.

Art

Shame is a funny thing. What if you hugged that bully and told him that he mattered and took a different approach? It is funny what affection does in place of humility. Since I don't have a loser stamp nor is ink for sale in this transaction, I hardly see how my poor stamps could be of help. Best wishes on your shame tactics, I am a get-them-with-kindness person!!!

24 Glass Test Tube 15 X 150mm heat resistant and bonus

This is an auction for 60 small test tube Stainless Caps—Size 13—1.5cm diameter. Brand new.

Greetings! While watching a rerun of *Charles in Charge* starring Scott Baio an idea popped into my head. I don't get out of the house much but love to experiment and mix chemicals in my basement. Using a combination of melted deodorant, hydroxy ethyl cellulose extract from hair gel, and cheap cologne with a dash of Tellurium (Te) just for kicks, I wish to create a new cologne for men entitled BAIO! I believe those elements would re-create the vibrant smell of the real life Chachi. I once stood behind him in line at a Redondo Beach Starbucks in 2004 and remember his distinct musky smell like it was just yesterday. I believe everyone will want to wear and smell like BAIO! in the future. I am looking for test tubes on eBay to help store my BAIO! concoctions. Could your test tubes withstand my ingredients heated to over 300 degrees Fahrenheit? How about sub-zero temps? Would the atomic weight of the Tellurium (Te) shatter the tubes? Thank you.

Art

Hello,

I'm so out of touch I'm not sure who this celebrity is. Can you even get Tellurium or any of its compounds?

Tellurium compounds are considered amongst the worst smelling compounds in the universe. Much worse than sulfur or phosphorous. I'm an organophosphate chemist, and I make a lot of sulfur derivatives. I have never smelled a tellurium compound but I have heard (and believe) this story.

A German chemist made some alkyltellurium compound in the late 1800's and was on a train when it fell out of his pocket. No matter what was done, the stink was so bad they had to abandon the entire coach forever. I got that story from *The Emperor of Scent,* which is a great book. I also suggest *The Chemistry of Fragrances* compiled by David H. Pybus and Charles S. Sell.

Cymbal Mallets—"For All Drum Set Players Stick Bag"

1 pr. Cymbal Mallets

Yarn Wound (White for Visibility) Rubber Core, 1/2" birch handles. More durable than felt mallets.

About Smith Mallets: 20 years ago I began making mallets while in college for myself as a hobby and also because name brand mallets are so very expensive. After a short time my fellow percussionist friends wanted me to make mallets for them which led to the start of "Smith Mallets." My business was marketed solely by word-of-mouth and in time the mallets made their way into the hands of students at many colleges and universities all over the country.

Greetings! Ever since I heard the catchy tune "Dr. Feel-good" by Mötley Crüe, I have been a huge fan of drummer Tommy Lee. The rhythm and syncopation he lays down is unmatched in the rock and roll world. Tommy is the king of drummers! Despite his bad boy reputation he is still a leader in his community as evidenced by his return to college and involvement with the inner city youth. He makes kites and peanut brittle for them. I am planning a tribute to Tommy by recording myself drumming on turtle shells. My uncle, Herman, runs a turtle farm and has graciously donated eight turtles to my project (loosely titled Hell on Shells). There's a tiny turtle named Gerry who will be my hi-hat. His father, Roger, is serving as the bass drum. After each session they will be rewarded with 3 heads of lettuce each. NO TURTLES WILL BE HARMED IN MY EVENT. Naturally, their shells are hard. Do you believe your great drumsticks will break upon impact? How many hits until the sticks start to wear down?

Art

Hi Art,

Thanks for telling me about your event. It sounds like a great time. I think the mallets will hold up fine. But they are made of birch and if you are really going to bash I could make some out of hickory. So let me know if you want the hickory and I'll be glad to do that for you.

Thanks,
Robb

ARROW VINTAGE COUNTIES JIGSAW PUZZLE; UK + Ireland

ARROW
JIGSAW
<u>Vintage Jigsaw map of THE UK & IRELAND</u>
It has ALL the pieces!

*This is a very collectible vintage jigsaw map from the 1970's.
It has a fascinating map of England, Wales, Scotland & Ire-
land, complete with all the counties + the Western Isles
It is an amazing piece of history for all collectors.*

<u>It has all the pieces & measures 20.5 inches by 15.5 inches</u>
<u>(52.1 x 39.4 cm)</u>

*It is made by Arrow & these were designed to be very educa-
tional as well as fun!*

300 pieces

Hello! I am in the middle of planning our family vacation to Europe and may have use for your European Map Puzzle. I am especially excited to visit the beautiful country of Poland as I recently discovered I have a third cousin named Frydryck Tomaszewski living there. He works in a Polish dog factory. We also plan on visiting England and the famous Stonehenge monument. I read that King Arthur sacrificed virgins there. That's something the kids might enjoy. Anyway, as we all know it's difficult to fold and unfold maps, I thought that I could glue your puzzle to a piece of cardboard. That way we would have a map of Europe that we wouldn't have to fold. Could we use your European Map Puzzle to navigate our way throughout Europe? Is it easy to see the names of roads and highways? Would glue even stick to your puzzle pieces?

Art

Hi

Well, you could glue it as it is cardboard but it does not show any roads. It shows regional things of that country—e.g., a skier/cuckoo clock in Switzerland. Handy to overcome the language barrier. You could just point to something you wanted. But don't buy a clock, it will drive you mad. This jigsaw map is also approx. 30 years old and even if it did show roads I think you would have a very challenging trip using out of date info! Also you asked this question on the Europe map but sent it via the England map listing. That doesn't show roads either but the countries are handy to see where you thought you should be instead of where you are. Assuming most of them are still here. With this government, they'll probably all get merged into the land of Blair soon. You'd be better off with a proper map for navigating (provided you have a degree in origami, you'll be fine), but the jigsaws would help you remember which country/county is where in relation to everything else.

Stonehenge—bunch of rocks in the middle of no-where built by neanderthals/aliens/whatever. (Depends on which fruitcake theory you subscribe to.) Not King Arthur. That's (supposedly) Tintagel in Cornwall. Nice place for a cream tea. Take an umbrella—oh heck, given our weather, bring full scuba gear. We have a drought order but it's done nothing but piddle with rain for the last month. We don't sunbathe, we go rusty. Suggest you also visit something like our fabulous secret nuclear bunker as that has typical directions on it for tourists. If you understand those, you're doing well. I've never been there. Have been to Stonehenge (you can't actually walk on it, as it's roped off)—God forbid someone may actually damage a large rock . . . hmmm large rock v small squishy human, I think I know what would suffer most . . . ho hum! Have also been to Tintagel. Scenic and very good cream teas. Enjoy your trip.

Persian Short Haired White Ceramic Kitty Cat Figurine

Does this look like anyone you know? Absolutely fabulous. How can you NOT love this face. Wow. Handcrafted, handpainted offering from the *Artisans,* dated 1989. Lovely, ceramic collectible figurine. Cold cast stone resin—sandstone. Original, handmade work of art. No two are alike, so you know that the one you receive is just as individual as your own kitty.

Does this look like your kitty? Meow. Your lovable Persian. ((S)he looks like a short haired exotic Persian or your sweet lovable white kitty.) Check out that super long tail. Those blue eyes!!

I love cats and I'm sure you do too. If this isn't the kitty you're looking for, be sure to check out other of my auctions, as I have Maine Coon, Tabby, Burmese and more.

3.5" x 3" x 1.5" (measurements are approximate)
1/4 of a lb.
Creamy white fur (hint/blush of color)
Bright Blue Eyes

One of my hobbies is quite unusual. I collect different ceramic animals and build what I like to call my "Fighting Brigades." I set up different figurines around my parents' basement and have them battle to the death! (Just last week the Flying Pigs of the 27th in an upset beat the Wolverines from Down Under.) The winner is decided by whoever's left standing by throwing Cheez-its from behind the couch. On special missions I use Oreo Cookies as grenades. I would think that your Ceramic Persian Cat would be a great addition to the Fabulous Felines. My questions: How solid is your figurine? I see that she is 3½ inches tall, which would be considered a pawn in my war. How many Cheez-its do you think it can withstand before it's blasted to smithereens? How about Oreos? Your description asks "Does this look like anyone you know?" Quite honestly it does look like my childhood cat, Fluffy, who mistimed her jump off a forklift and well, you know.

Art

Hey—I'm crazy about pigs, so their win, for me, is outstanding. This kitty is solid and weighs right at 8 ounces. Fairly hefty for its size. I think it could withstand a Cheez-it onslaught and feel fairly certain that it would take a barrage of Oreos (or a few VERY stale) to do any serious damage. I didn't have either of those handy, so I tossed a few shelled peanuts in the general direction and nada.

Sorry to hear about Fluffy—she obviously wasn't cut out for construction work. Let me know if you have any more questions. I do have other of the feline figurines if you're interested.

Have a great day!
Dimitre

POWDER HORN Revolutionary War Flintlock Reenactment Gun

Powder horn

Our powder horns, replicating Revolutionary War period pieces, are crafted in genuine cowhorn, with hardwood caps and stoppers. Three styles are available. Ideal for the reenactor or mountain man persona. Three styles are available. Made from cowhorn.

Hello! My fifth grade class is currently studying the Revolutionary War and I plan on adding some pizzazz to the curriculum. They are having some trouble understanding all the details of the war, though. Therefore, I am going to dress as Abraham Lincoln and recite his famous "I Have a Dream" speech to the class in an American accent. I will tell stories of how the Germans occupied that one country in Europe and how we (America) overthrew that one really bad guy. I will discuss how the British (U.K., United Kingdom, England, Whales, etc.) invented the grenade and how they bombed those ships in the harbor that were holding tea and coffee. If you didn't know, that was called "The Boston Tea Party Massacre." Remember, I'll be dressed up and talk like the great war hero Abraham Lincoln. My students will love it! Your Powder Horn would be a great addition to my presentation. How easy would it be to play a song like "Taps" or "Revely" on it? I used to play the saxophone. Does it in any way sound like a conch shell? Thank you.

Art

Hi Art,

I am so glad to hear that the school system is finally taking hold of the lack of education here in America, and teaching the real facts. This Powder Horn isn't tuned very well, but we do offer this great big thing called a "Horn Cornu" that was made by the Romans and sounds like an elephant. You can still play the Powder Horn if you'd like, but you would need to drill a couple holes if you want to get "Taps" out of it. We don't offer this as a service, unfortunately. Please let me know if you have any more questions.

Best regards,

Leon

Tennis Rackets / Squash Rackets new RacquetSlugger New

Hello and happy day to you! I wish to tell you up front how I would use your tennis racket. You see, my older brother, Lawrence, was extremely abusive to me growing up. Out on our farm he would throw rocks at my head, make me eat hay, squirt goat milk in my eye, and once purposely lit my toes on fire. Rocky relationship to say the least! There is a huge family reunion on December 8 (town hall) and I am planning the ultimate revenge. When Lawrence walks in with his trophy wife (he loves a grand entrance) a racket of some sorts will be placed above the door. I will rig it to a spring and then KA-BOOM! the racket will snap down into his face with the force of a medieval catapult. Everyone will laugh and mock him and point fingers! It will be my revenge. (I will have a clown armed with pies as my backup plan.) My questions: How tight are the strings on your racket? If I apply 25 pounds of pressure to the springs how much damage could it do? Could it break a human nose?

Art

Art,

I can sympathize with you. Except my brother was my mom's favorite. I heard through my childhood why can't you be more like your brother? He is now in prison and I still hear the same thing—why can you be more like your brother? My brother dropped a concrete block off a 2-story window onto my head. It only broke the block in 3 pieces. I have a hard head.

Sure, I understand the amusing prank but I do hope it wouldn't break his nose. I guess if it hit the racket part it could, but I think that everyone mocking him and laughing would do more damage to the human pride than the breaking the nose part.

I say play the joke but don't seriously hurt the guy. Also, set up an array of assorted pranks throughout the day. Well planned would produce great revenge.

Good luck!!! Let me know how it works out.

Ron

Ben Nye Super White Professional Face Powder

Non-translucent, blended with white pigment to brighten any white makeup including Clown White, Clown White Lite or foundations such as Geisha and Porcelain.

Hello! I have a secret that I'm going to reveal to my family. You see, in the middle of the night I like to dress as a mime. I practice my mime activities in front of the mirror such as "Trapped in Glass Box," "The King Tut" and "The Robot." My roommate almost caught me once, but I ducked behind my dresser. My parents are hosting a dinner party in three weeks and I will literally come out of the closet dressed as a mime and reveal my true self. (As a token of goodwill I might make animal balloons.) I'm not ashamed of being a mime—that's who I am. I've always used Aubrey Organics face powder to completely cake my face in white but recently it's left a nasty rash on my face. I need a new face powder. Would your face powder cause a rash on my face? My face oil level is a category 4. Will it last on my face over a five-hour period before disintegrating? I don't know how long I'm going to be in the closet. Thank you.

Art

Hi

Sorry I didn't answer you earlier—I have a new e-mail and your question went to the junk mail folder (which I just discovered). I am not sure what Category 4 oil level is. I myself have very oily skin (most foundations cream off of my face within a couple of hours) and I have quite sensitive skin (can't use most shampoos, conditioners, washing powders, etc.). I can wear this powder without it creaming off and running and I have no problems with skin sensitivity. It isn't a foundation but it gives a nice pale complexion and is great over foundation. Whatever your decision with the powder, good luck with your family.

Thanks
Dana

NWT Juicy Couture Athletic Sweat Velour Pajama Suit L

Juicy Couture Athletic Sweat Suit

Style: 95% Cotton, 5% Cotton, VELOUR, Stretch
Waist
Condition: New with tags
Size: Petite Large (L)
Color: Black
Retail: $220.00
Please Note: Juicy Couture Sweat Suits are made
in PETITE sizes, and run small. PLEASE check
measurements!

Hello! I currently hold a master's degree in Eastern Philosophy from Cornell University and am, naturally, fascinated by the book *The Da Vinci Code*. Despite my higher education level I am without a job, as I failed to get my multi-level-marketing business, called Spamway, off the ground. Anyway, as one who has also immersed himself in the hip-hop culture, I wish to write my first novel, entitled *Da Fa Shizzle Hizzle Code*. The plot will revolve around a character named Sir Fo Hizzie Nizzie and how he must solve a murder mystery by deciphering an enigmatic riddle found in a rap song. In a breathless race through Compton, the Bronx, and Austin, Texas, they must match wits with a Caucasian-faced record executive who may be part of a secret society called The Blue Oyster Cult. I'm looking to buy some velour sweats on eBay to "get me in the hip-hop mood" when I type my novel. How much do you think I would perspire in your velour sweats? I am considered a heavy sweater and am in the 99th percentile. Thank you.

Art

Hi Art,

Thanks for your inquiry, and best of luck on your book. Juicy Couture is considered more high-end than "ghetto" in terms of its target market. You might want to pursue Baby Phat or Rocawear sweat suits. The amount you would perspire in this sweat suit would most likely depend on the temperature of your environment, the type of physical activity you endured while wearing it, and the amount of fluid in your body. All of this assuming, of course, you could fit into the suit, as these are women's juicy's suits.

Poetry—*A Night Without Armor*
by Jewel Kilcher (1998)

This book of poetry is in very good condition. This is Jewel's first book of poems. This gal has used her words in a search for truth and meaning and has used them to record, discover and reflect. She writes of home, family and even the beauty of Alaska. The Alaska connection is how I came upon this book but these poems show images of the road, faraway places and many more experiences.

Greetings! My town is conducting a poetry contest with a grand prize of $200 and I am currently working on material for submission. My love for poetry started in 1978 when my fifth grade teacher, Ms. Buxbaum, encouraged me in poetry writing. I have never looked back. My first poem was simply titled "Mother's Milk." I'm currently working on two poems but am having difficulty with the endings. I figured Jewel's book of poetry could lend a hand in this process. "The more one reads, the more one learns" is my motto. I'm willing to share my two poems with you.

> *I listen to the elk*
> *I hear their cry*
> *My heart yearns for them*
> *They do neat stuff*
> *Like make pelts and jerky*

And my second one:

> *How high are the mountains?*
> *I cannot tell*
> *How about water fountains?*
> *They shoot water in my eye*

Do you believe your book of poetry could help me finish my poems? There's no way I could copy some lines from Jewel's book, is there? Could you possibly send some constructive criticism my way? Thank you.

Art

On the first poem—they do neat stuff like make pelts and jerky just doesn't seem to work. How about something about their morning breath in the cold mountain air, their majestic calls as they graze in a meadow, and there is always: if I could see through their eyes the world they abound in . . . course that's if you want a serious poem. If you want the chuckle and quick kind I kind of like your finish about pelts and jerky. Jewel's book is cute—some of the poems read like a story. Maybe that's a true poem—tell a story in a few lines. And although you can't copy her thoughts or lines, they might get you to thinking about your short clips in life to make a poem from. Send me the one you submit to the contest. Good luck.

PS—the water fountain one is funny and cute—to my mind they are like waterfalls and so maybe change to how high are the mountains and their waterfalls? I cannot tell. How about water fountains? They shoot water in my eye.

Shure T Series SM58 Hand Held Wireless Microphone

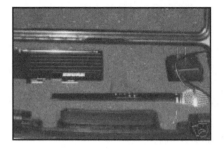

Although this mic is used, it has less than one hour use. It is a professional model with mic stand holder. It comes with the user guide that has never been opened. It is approximately 10 inches in length. It cost $250.00 new and it's in like new condition now. For an extra $25 dollars, I'll sell you the mic stand with boom (like new, if still available). Be sure to check out my other head-set mic up for bid also. I also have speakers and power/pre amps for sale.

Hi! I consider myself an entrepreneur of sorts who has dabbled in such inventions as The Ambidextrous Toothbrush, Fake Doggy-Doo in a Can and BAIO! Cologne for Men. I was recently approached by a friend (let's call him Donny) with an idea that sounds too good to be true. He's a third cousin to Charlton Heston's agent and wants to partner up with me in exploring a new business venture. We would produce a CD of the chiseled jawed man reading aloud the rap lyrics of Tupac Shakur, Ice-T, and Snoop Dogg in dramatic fashion—as only he can. We would call it *Charlton Heston: Rollin' with the Gangstas*. There's a German investor named Hans who's VERY interested in financially backing us. We are meeting Mr. Heston in two weeks and want to sample some of his readings. We have a PX-78 soundboard but need a microphone. How far away from his mouth should Mr. Heston put your microphone to pick up every syllable or phrase like "glock in yo' face"? Maybe four inches? He has a booming voice. He was Moses for Pete's sake! Thank you.

Art

Hey Art, if you're making a professional CD in a studio you wouldn't need my mic at all. The wireless mic is better for live performances not for professional recording. A studio would have the mics necessary, along with wind screens so that one's breath would not be picked up on the recording. Even if you are recording the CD in your own home, I would recommend that you purchase a professional mic with a cord. This will transmit the voice better and with less possibility of cracking. Good luck. Mark

Kendo Shinai Bamboo Practice Sword Iaido Samurai Boken

Nakaoji Knife & Martial Arts Supply

The shinai is a traditional practice weapon used in kendo. Perfect way to practice sword handling safely. Split bamboo construction with an adjustable leather collar and a leather-wrapped handle. Comes with a hard plastic collar guard and rubber retaining ring. Sword measures 42 inches overall. The more you buy, the more you save. Other practice swords available; please see our other auctions!

Hello! I manage a nonprofit clinic where we rehabilitate chimpanzees that were rejected by their mothers and place them back into the wild. Last year we offered to donate Sunny to the San Diego Zoo but they respectfully declined due to her category 5 PTT (Poop Throwing Tendencies). We teach these delicate creatures survival skills. It's a jungle out there! Last month we hired a professional boxer to teach them to throw a punch. They used gloves—don't worry! A local high school wrestling coach showed them the proper way to put another chimp in a Full Nelson position. The next skill we will teach them is how to use a Bamboo Shinai properly. We are looking to buy sticks for the chimps to spar with. Naturally, chimpanzees possess opposable thumbs which they can use to grip the swords with. But, we're concerned that Kelli won't be able to fit her hands around the handle. Her tiny digits are around one inch long. Will she be able to grip your sword? Thank you.

Art

Hi,

Thank you for the question. Sorry I have not been able to get back to you sooner, I have been busy training (with humans that is). The shinai that we have would be too large for the chimps. We can order the mini shinai, but do not have any in stock. This is what we use in our 1 and 2 year olds sword fighting classes. Also you will need our custom-made helmet, gloves, chest protector, cup, mouth piece, goggles, head band, leg protectors, sword carrying case and special instructor training. Please do not attempt to do this until you get the training, which will take between 2 and 5 years. You would probably be better off teaching jiu jitsu which requires no equipment other than a custom made gi. Good luck in your quest. BTW, you should probably contact the local high school, as the full nelson is illegal in high school wrestling.

Large Wooden Rocking Horse Ride On Wood Toy 37½" Tall

This is a great rocking horse that we are selling.
Please click each picture to get the best view.
The rocking horse is wooden.
Seat is padded a little too.
It is 37½" high and 43" long and 14¼" wide
runners on the bottom are screwed in
with phillips head.
My 4 year old grandson can easily fit on it
and ride on it.

Hello! Go ahead and call me nuts but I'm looking to break a Guinness World Record by riding on a rocking horse for 48 hours straight. I was inspired by the episode of *The Brady Bunch* when Bobby and Cindy tried to break the world record riding on a teeter totter. Two years ago I attempted a similar stunt in which I clung to a fire pole for 4 hours (MAJOR chafing). In the event I fall asleep on the horse, I will not be disqualified if the horse continues to rock. Once the horse comes to a complete halt the clock stops. (Adriano Fuchela from Italy currently holds the record at 43 hours.) During the course of this attempt I will be viewing season one of *Wonder Woman* staring Linda Carter, listening to John Tesh CDs, and crocheting a beautiful baby blue and pink bonnet for my niece Julie-Ann. I have acquired Rainbow Bread as a sponsor. Do you believe your rocking horse can hold me (6 foot 4, 165 lbs.) rocking on it for 48 hours? I don't see footholds for my size 17 shoes. Suggestions? Thank you.

Art

I just went down and rode on it myself. I unfortunately am much shorter than you and weigh even a little more. Not even a creak in it. Works great. I put my feet on the rungs when I rode it. That is where you should put them. Now, my feet are far from 17's. The thickness of the body, head, legs are 1 and 1/2 inches thick. Boards on runners are 1 inch thick. It is put together with screws and the legs are fastened with a metal band holding it together. There is a very good chance this will hold up. My husband says if you do this you have to send us a picture. I love John Tesh though. I might be able to rock for quite some time just listening to him. But never watch TV, crochet and listen to music while rocking. You are very talented.

Hard hat with
2 terry cloth liners

This is a like-new Hard Hat with 2 two sweat liners.
It is a Van Guard. Any questions please e-mail me.

Hello! I am searching eBay for a hard hat to wear during my job as a city bus driver. As I'm sure you're aware of, construction hard hats are tough to come by. The black market was a logical choice but my contact came up dry. I need some type of protective headgear due to the constant jeering and physical abuse I encounter on a daily basis. Basically, I work in gang-infested territories where I have been pelted by objects from ten-pound bricks to fresh fruit (bananas and tomatoes are their favorites). To get an idea think *The Warriors* meets the movie *Speed.* The reason I have yet to quit or file a complaint is due to the wonderful 401K plan and complimentary danish rolls the city provides. I have, though, struck up an unlikely friendship with someone called The Brainsmasher. This may sound somewhat frivolous but can your hard hat deflect objects (batteries, crow bars, etc.) thrown by hooligans from ten to twenty feet away? Also, would your hard hat impair my vision of the road? Thank you very much.

Art

I hope that 401K is really great! This is a like-new hard hat. It was made for construction workers. Safety tested and all. Of course I think your job would really put it thru the tests. You should not have any problem driving with this hat on and you can adjust it to fit your head just right. And just in case you break a sweat, you have the 2 terry cloth liners to catch the sweat! If this hard hat doesn't work I suggest you ask Uncle Sam for a combat helmet.

Thanks, Ann

New Lafayette Drafting Studio Chair w/Loop

Lafayette Drafting Chair

The Lafayette Series provides for a quality range of seating at an affordable price. Equipped with a spacious seat and back and basic ergonomics.

Features:
- Contoured backrest: 16"w 10"h
- Back vertical height adjustment range: 3.5"
- Contoured backrest with lumbar support
- Ergonomically contoured seat: 17"w 15"d
- Pneumatic cylinder, vertical mode adjustment: 24"–33"
- 5-Star reinforced plastic diameter base: 23"
- Hooded dual-wheel carpet casters
- Teardrop footrest
- Assembly required

Let me be frank here, I want to duct tape myself to a rolling chair and be pushed from the top of a small hill. My reason is quite simple—I want to live the good life and bankrupt my current employer. I work for an investment firm where the working conditions are awful. They brew stale coffee, make us work over 75 hours a week with no overtime, and Fred (a snotty investor) secretly stapled a 3 X 5 card that read "Brokeback Mountain" to the back of my jacket. Anyway, my friend Brice Coker has agreed to push me, duct taped to a chair, from the top of a grassy hill on our business's property. Legal law says that a business is liable for all expenses when injuries occur on business property. I figure I will sustain some broken bones and hopefully a few internal injuries (big payout). I'm crossing my fingers, hoping for a financially productive concussion. Would duct tape hold firm to your drafting chair? If I chicken out, is there an easy way to stop your chair? Thank you.

Art

To return your honesty, using this chair for your plan would put your future in the hands of fate or at least in the reliability of Chinese manufacturing—if you don't believe in fate. Alas, as a gifted customer service representative, I offer other advice. About Fred, I think it's safe to say he may have secret feelings towards you; watch closely in the next few days. Grade school children, unable to verbalize their emotions, often pester the kids they have crushes on. On to your plan: It's clever, but you've missed a few details. Of course it all depends on if your small hill has a drainage ditch or a grassy parking lot divider. Regardless, if you are duct-taped to the chair, most of your injuries would be sustained to the head and maybe the lower legs. The bulk of your body and arms would be protected by the chair. So I suggest wearing a helmet to avoid head injuries, and I would consider using twist ties instead of tape. That way you can tie your hands behind the chair and your legs to the outside part of the chair, increasing the possibility of damaged or broken limbs significantly. Plus, the ties can be removed and discarded whereas the duct tape would surely leave residue: evidence of your scheme. Trust me, insurance claim inspectors can be ruthlessly perceptive. Good luck to you and please keep me posted on the results of your endeavor.

Sincerely, Jason

Wooly Bugger—30 New Assorted Fly Fishing Flies LOT

This is a very versatile pattern that will catch fish on virtually any lake, pond or river. The success this fly has enjoyed over the years is due to its life-like action, provided by the palmered hackle and soft marabou tail. The wooly bugger streamer fly (some books call this fly a nymph) was probably the very first fly I ever used (and caught a fish with). It, undoubtedly, is the most popular streamer pattern made; I would assume just about every fly fisherman has a variety of colors and hook sizes in their fly box. This fly is a deadly representation of a leech and many other types of food that fish find attractive.

Hello! I have had a three year running issue with my neighbor, George Gilmore, and it's time to take the offensive! He has thrown palm branches into my yard, mortally wounded the family cat with a wild lawn dart, and sun bathes (in Speedo) with Neil Diamond music blaring. He is a bad man. Once, he threw a cigarette across our fence which engulfed my rose bushes in flames. He's like a cop or a security guard or a mailman so I haven't filed an official complaint yet. I'm very handy with a fly rod and hope to turn the tables and cause havoc in the life of George Gilmore. During the night hours I will stand on a two foot ladder and steal items from George Gilmore's back yard using a fly rod. I will lift the following items: his trusty sun bathing towel, his BBQ brush, his pet parrot (caged), and his 8-track collection. Do you believe your Wooly Buggers would be able to latch onto a parrot? If so, are they strong enough to completely lift the bird out of its cage and across his lawn? Thank you.

Art

I'm not sure if you are serious. The fisherman would have to be quite accurate with the fly rod to attach a fly to the parrot. Not sure what test tippet you would need, but I assume if the parrot was to fly it could be a pretty good battle. David

White House Black Market
Black & White Poncho L

This poncho was a gift and has never been worn. It is from White House Black Market. It is very, very soft. It has a cowl neck and fringe all around the bottom. This is a great new item at used prices.

Greetings! As assistant director of theatre at Martin Luther Middle School (the famous protestant reformer), a dream of mine has been realized. You see, I have written a play entitled *Pancho Villa and the Amazing Technicolor Poncho*. The play will revolve around the Mexican vigilante Pancho Villa and will showcase colorful ponchos that he and his gang, Division del Norte, wore during their terrible raids in the early 1900s. It will be spectacular as the actors will parade around in colorful cloaks and ponchos, acting out various types of pillages and plunders. The songs will include "Gringos Smingos." "We Don't Need No Stinkin' Badges," and "Woodrow Wilson Is a Weenie." People will love it! I have secured many Mexican bearded actors, borrowed six horses, and a wonderful seamstress named Bonnie has donated her time. Your poncho looks lovely. Would Bonnie be able to easily sew rainbow colors into the fabric? Would it fit a slender 13-year-old boy named Christopher (Pancho Villa)? Thank you.

Art

This sounds like a great accomplishment and I would love for my poncho to be a part of the wonderful show. The material is acrylic and is either knitted or crocheted. I would think that it would be quite simple to add colors anywhere you choose. As for the size, I am not sure if it will work. I will give you the measurements and let you be the judge. The length is 18 inches to the bottom not including the fringe. The width is 26 inches and the material is very stretchy. I would think that this would work without overwhelming Christopher. Good Luck!!

80 bendy straws BNIB

80 x bendy straws. Brand new.

Please check out my e-shop for more great value items. Happy bidding!

Greetings! I have an unusual hobby and am searching eBay for new straws. You see, I enter high school football games and fire spitballs at unsuspecting cheerleaders. I hide behind trash cans, mingle with the band, and once donned football garb for a closer shot. Once, in 2003, a perfectly placed spit wad made eye contact with head cheerleader Missy DeGroot. This week St. Lucy of Arcadia is playing Mission Prep and my partner in crime, Marcus, and I have scouted out the area. We're going to hide under the bleachers. In high school, cheerleaders and their boyfriends routinely mocked Marcus and I. It wasn't odd to hear such phrases as "New pimple today, huh, Art? What's that make now—142?," "Hey Marcus, finish my homework or else you'll be seeing the bottom of the toilet again!" and "Look who's walking toward us—the Hump Brothers." Now we shoot spit wads at them. How thick are your straws? In your opinion, would they make excellent weapons?

Art

And greetings to you Art! I hope Missy DeGroot made a full recovery and hasn't been scarred for life. The straws are 5mm across. Would that fit your optimum wad dimensions? Do you think the bend in them will make it difficult to aim satisfactorily with? Or maybe it would mean you could aim around corners, thereby escaping detection and being able to blame people in more obvious fire range. I've had a thought—the straws are mostly white with different coloured stripes. You could colour-coordinate the straws with the team's colours! Or with your outfit, to help camouflage the wad weapon. I wish you luck with your hobby. Say hi to Marcus from me. Happy bidding, Sarah.

VIKING horned helmet, thor, norse, valkyrie

This is a vintage children's HORNED VIKING HELMET, identical to the one worn by the Thor-loving teen in the 80s movie *Adventures in Babysitting*! Perfect for a retro costume party!

The helmet is made of a gray plastic and features a gold plastic molding of a bird of prey. This item is in VERY GOOD condition with little wear considering its age.

It is an oft-cited fact that Vikings did not actually wear horned or winged helmets. However, the horn-style captures a mythical intensity not evoked by the conical and Wenceslas designs, although they may be more historically accurate. Wagner's *Der Ring des Nibelungen* is inspiring fantasy!

This might also be fun for LARP (NERO?) and boffing tournaments! How about some Valkyrie Profile horseplay? Starring in your very own Opera!?

You should probably buy this helmet.

Summer is upon us and our Over 40 Marco Polo League is about to begin. Our rules are quite unusual and we may need your viking helmet. This isn't your kid-friendly Marco Polo game—this is serious business. Every team appoints one player to be their "Berserker." The Berserker swims around and disrupts the person yelling "Marco" in any way they see fit. For the past three years Biff (6' 4", 295 lbs.) has been our Berserker and this year he chose a cattle prod as his disrupter. Last year he used an air horn. The year before, a fishing rod. Unfortunately, a teammate was injured by the cattle prod in a practice game and we're looking for a new disrupter for Biff. Apparently, people don't like to be prodded. First of all, is your viking helmet waterproof? Second, are the horns sharp enough to penetrate skin or would someone simply feel a slight poke? And finally, in your opinion, would it stay on Biff when he swims underwater? Thanks.

Art

I'm excited about this! I would surmise that the helmet is waterproof since it is entirely made of plastic materials. However, it will probably not stay on Biff's head as he dives underwater unless you come up with a manner of fastening it to his head, perhaps with a chin-strap. The horns are not sharp at all. They come to a dull point. I also need to warn you that the helmet is made of flexible plastic and will possibly tear or bend if it is subject to excessive force. If the helmet is fastened to Biff's head, he will be able to headbutt without fear of injury to others, but the helmet itself is another story. If you're only looking to use it for this one event then I would say go for it, but not if you plan on using it again and again for this purpose.

**WATER BOMB SLINGSHOT Balloon Launcher
TOY & 75 Balloons**

JUMBO WATER BOMB <u>SLINGSHOT</u>!!
SUPER LAUNCHING POWER!
Just Like They Use at the Stadiums ~
Launch Water Balloons,
T-Shirts and More!
**Includes slingshot w/hose adapter and
75 Balloons**

<u>Directions:</u>
1. One person holds one side handle.
2. Another person holds the other side handle.
*3. The 3rd person places the filled water balloon
into the sling, pulls back, and lets go to launch
the water balloon.*

Hello! I recently won a radio contest by eating 14 pounds of squid tentacles with caramel butter sauce and received a free hot air balloon ride. I am searching eBay for the best water balloon launcher to take with me. I can choose one person to ride with me and have chosen my metrosexual roommate, Jeff Bowden. We love to play pranks on our friends and create all sorts of mischief. I once set up over 300 clown puppets in the sanctuary of a church for my sister's wedding day! She hates clowns! When Jeff Bowden and I are high up in the hot air balloon we think it would be hilarious if we shot water balloons at houses, people at the park, and corporate offices (such as Starbucks). Your launcher looks perfect. How far back would we have to pull to launch a water balloon from a hot air balloon suspended 400 feet in the air? How accurate is your launcher? If we rose to 600 feet, in your opinion, would it be difficult to peg a hand-holding couple walking in the park? Thank you.

Art

Congrats on your win! Sounds like a ton of fun. The water bomb launcher requires 3 people. You know that, correct? You might be able to get away with hanging one side on some type of post or something, but it may affect the accuracy. Honestly, I don't know if you could hit a couple from 400 feet up, while moving. With practice, you should be able to get pretty accurate with this. Of course wind, the unevenness of the water balloon, the moving hot air balloon would also affect accuracy. Like I said, I would do lots of practice ahead of time. Even in the stadiums, when they shoot T-shirts into the stands and such, without a lot of practice, they're not going to hit a particular seat. More like a section. Hope that helps.

Buescher Trumpet made in USA - Used

Trumpet comes in original case. Has two (2) mouth-pieces, one (1) mute and attaching sheet music holder.

This unit is used and has a few dents. Great starter trumpet. Could even be used as a decoration!
Valves need oil.

Greetings! Last year I tried my hand at the bass drum and auditioned for the Swinging Crows Community Band. I practiced long hours banging a homemade bass drum made from wax paper, Wrigley's Double Mint Gum and an old "worry free" wire birdcage. My wife, Edna, grew quite tiresome about my practice habits and once hurled an old shoe (Reebok) at me that bloodied my left ear. My tryout in front of Maestro Robert M. Ferguson didn't fare well as he stated, "Art, you played like a wild kangaroo on steroids. I'm sorry, we can't have you in the band. You can try out again next year." I was devastated. I plan on trying out again for the SCCB. This time on trumpet. Since childhood I have had the uncanny ability to blow very fast air through my nose. I may sound crazy but do you believe I could play the trumpet through my nose rather than my lips? I believe I could generate a better tone and sound that way. Would your trumpet mouthpiece be able to fit around my left nostril? Thank you.

Art

Well! In order to answer I need to know the size of your left nostril. I will then compare your nose size to my brother and I will attempt to make him blow. Pictures are always good. Thank you for your interest. The listing was worth your question.

Dr. James Dobson on Parenting NEW
Book Focus on Family

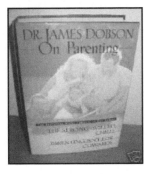

Dr. James Dobson on Parenting

Two Bestselling Works Complete in One Volume

The Strong-Willed Child
Parenting Isn't for Cowards

502 pages, Hardcover, New, 1997, Inspirational Press.

CONDITION: New

Practical parenting advice that really works—from America's foremost family counselor!

Help! Our four-year-old son, Ishmael, is out of control and is starting to exhibit some anti-social behaviors. Perhaps your Dobson book could give us some parenting tips. Just last week we took Ishmael to the mall and he pushed over 14 kids, stole a lady's wallet (Versace), and pelted a Hot Dog on a Stick worker with a mustard-laced corn dog. We've always provided the best for Ishmael and don't know why he's become so mean spirited and spoiled. Granted, my wife Norma occasionally breast feeds him when he asks for his "nummies," but we figure that's fairly normal. That's what our spiritual adviser says. He would know, he has 3 wives and 22 children. Anyway, is there a chapter in the Dobson book that deals with four-year-old boys who still breast feed and throw corn dogs at mall workers? How about advice when Ishmael screams, "I hate you, Mommy! I wish you were never born!" or "Can't you do anything right, Daddy? You're so stupid!" I sure hope so. Thank you.

Art

Hi Art,

Sounds like you've got your hands full with Ishmael. As I flipped through the *James Dobson on Parenting* book I was surprised to find not a single chapter devoted to demon-possessed children. Since I don't have children myself, I went looking for help. Your situation was intriguing and aside from making a video and sending it in to *Nanny 911* or a licensed adolescent psychotherapist, I have compiled a list of 5 books you can obtain elsewhere that may prove effective. I hope it helps.

Understanding Mental Retardation by Patricia Ainsworth
Primer for Parents of Slow Children by Jackie Wright
Forced Exit: The Slippery Slope from Assisted Suicide to Legalized Murder by Wesley J. Smith
Straight Talk about Psychiatric Medications for Kids, Revised Edition by Timothy E. Wilens
Stupid Things Parents Do to Mess Up Their Kids: Don't Have Them If You Won't Raise Them by Laura Schlessinger

Kids BMX Bike

Item is used, but in good operating condition with very good tires, and good overall appearance. It could however use a new set of pedals. From ground to top of frame (where the seat post goes into the frame) is 15 inches. Winning bidder can pick item up in the Elkhart, Indiana, area, or have it shipped for actual cost plus a three-dollar fee.

Hello! I am attempting a stunt inspired by the classic *Happy Days* episode where Fonzie jumps over a shark on water skis. Using a small vehicle (as I'm a mere 86 lbs.), I will jump across Devil's Alley located in Ojai, California. I will start at the top of a 40-foot ramp, reach a speed of 25 mph, and execute a jump 37 feet long. There will be quail feathers and bubble wrap on the canyon floor (28 feet down) to soften the blow should I fall. For added suspense, 55 tarantula spiders will be dispersed among the quail feathers. I will be wearing umpire gear to insure my safety. In 2003, I ventured to jump over Yosemite Creek using 15 trampolines, to no avail. I broke my thorax in four places. Five videographers will be filming my stunt, which will be sent to the Discovery Channel for their show *Midget Stunts: The Bigger the Better.* I love your bike and think it would fit my minuscule body perfectly. Would it smash to bits if it tumbled 28 feet down? Could I install a roll bar for extra safety? Thank you.

Art

Art, I can greatly appreciate what you have planned, as I am an avid sportbiker and have been in a few stunting videos and wrecks involving injury myself. Therefore I am sure you understand that I can accept no responsibility for how you choose to use this bike. This is a sturdy bike. I see no reason it would not make it through a 28-foot tumble without any severe damage, but I can make no guarantees. Any modifications made for safety are always a good idea if performed correctly. I wish you luck whatever you decide to do with the bike. Please understand that I cannot be held liable for your decisions concerning the bike's use. Let me know if you may be interested in exchanging some videos. Thanks.

New RavX Bicycle Tire Pump!
Bike Presta/Schrader

This is a new RavX Econo X Mini Pump.
RavX describes this pump as follows:
- Dual-valve swivel head
- Single-action stroke
- Soft kraton T-handle
- Composite barrel
- Lightweight
- Velcro strap & mounting bracket
- Max pressure: 120 PSI
- Alloy pins

Greetings! I'll admit that I'm a bit of an experimenter. Once, I attached a pair of self-made Bat-Wings to myself and jumped off my neighbor's (George Gilmore) roof. I suffered minor cuts and a bruised ego. Yesterday, a crazy idea popped into my brain when I was sipping on a latte from Starbucks. I'm addicted to the stuff and have wondered what it would feel like if I had Starbucks latte injected directly into my bloodstream. Then I thought of the perfect instrument to help do so—a bicycle pump. I used to own one but they stole it. Perhaps I could fill your bicycle pump with a Starbucks latte (no cream or sugar) and literally "pump" that sweet nectar right into my arm or leg (not my neck). I figure the pumping action will help procure my caffeine fix quicker. How difficult would it be to rig your bicycle pump so I could fill it with a Starbucks latte? Could I unscrew the top and pour the lukewarm liquid in? Could I attach a hypodermic needle for easier skin penetration? Thank you.

Art

Hello Art and thanks for your question.

First, it is the official position of LinearSpeed that one should not use any of our products in any way that penetrates the skin, or plays any part in a procedure involving a through-skin procedure. Further, our stuff just ain't that clean!

However, if you were so inclined, a bicycle pump could be used to aid in creating additional pressure if required. Although I am not one to discourage a sale, I must ponder if the additional pressure, or complexity, of the pump is needed.

Could you not just put the latte into an IV bag and take it as a drip while sitting and reading the paper or working on your computer?

The Management at LinearSpeed.com

Nina Lyman dogs by Nina— Siberian Husky Vase

You are bidding on a terrific piece by artist "Nina Lyman."
This is one of Nina's famous ceramic puppy vases
of a **"SIBERIAN HUSKY."** This beautiful, blue-eyed
Husky stands 8½" tall and has an opening in the back
for flowers. Looks great without the flowers too! ~~
SO CUTE! This vase is stamped on the bottom "Nina
Lyman, Dogs by Nina" and is artist signed on the back
"Dogs by Nina." Item is brand new, has never been
used or displayed, and it is in perfect condition.

What a sad but great find I have made here on eBay! First a short story before my question: At the age of 13 years old I was given a husky dog by my Great Uncle Herbert. I named him Spanky. I loved my dog as much as my own family members. (He even made 2nd call for the classic Disney film *Iron Will*.) Tragically he was struck by lightning and then was hit by an ice cream truck while I flagged it down. (Strawberry Push-Ups were his favorite.) Is there a possibility that your Siberian Husky Vase could be painted to have a Fu Manchu on his hindquarters? Silly I know, but Spanky had a birthmark shaped like a Fu Manchu there. If I bid and win your fine auction, do you believe it would be difficult for me to personally paint it? The resemblance of your auction and my former 1st mate are uncanny and this would be a great memento of the happiest time of my life. Thanks for your time.

Art

Hello Art,

Thank you for sharing that wonderful story about your Husky, Spanky. I really enjoyed reading what you wrote. As far as painting the vase goes . . . I would guess that could be done. After all, it is ceramic and ceramics are made to be painted. However, I would guess that the portion you paint would have a different gloss as the rest of the piece. I'm sure there's a way you could paint a clear gloss over that and perhaps match the glossy finish on the remainder, but I can't promise, as I've never gone ahead and tried. Either way, it is a terrific piece and I'm sure you won't be disappointed.

Laura

Cat Tree Scratcher House Post Furniture Condo Meow 175

DESCRIPTION

- *High quality wood construction*
- **Overall Dimension: 12" L X 12" W X 24" H**
- *Hanging toy included*
- *Easy to assemble, step by step instruction*
- *No tools required, just a pair of hands*
- **Base Plate and Platform are thick and stable**
- **Scratching Post is made of 100% natural sisal rope**
- **Posts are all 3.5" diameter and wrapped with 1/4" sisal rope**
- **Available Color: beige**

Hello! I am a chimney sweep who lives in a modest studio apartment. When I come home from work covered in soot and scum I love being greeted by my cats. I've named them The Huxtable Family, after the characters from the hit sitcom *The Cosby Show.* There's Dr. Huxtable, Clair, Sondra, Denise, Theodore, Vanessa, and of course little Rudy (Siamese). Theodore is my favorite. He's such a cuddle muffin! Sondra is very stubborn, just like her TV character. Lately, I've been overwhelmed due to lack of space and their spraying rituals. I thought of building a hotel-like structure for them to play and live in, but I have no hammer. Do you believe the top layer could be made into an OB-GYN office complete with fiber-optic lighting systems and clamps just like Bill Cosby's? I know Dr. Huxtable would love it! (He doesn't like to be called Cliff.) Is there room for the bottom floor to serve as the family kitchen? The Huxtables need a nice place to dwell and your cat house could be the answer. Thank you.

Art

Art,

Thanks for your interests in our products.

I am not sure what is the meaning of OB-GYN? I doubt it will be enough space for all the Huxtables to dwell in the bottom floor, the box is about 12X12 only. Let me know if you need further info. By the way, how much do you charge for chimney sweep? Our fireplace is in the basement and last year when we tried to use the fireplace, the smoke seems that it can't go through the chimney. Maybe a nest of something up top, how much would that roughly cost me?

Incredible Hulk Hands Smashing Sounds Boxing Gloves

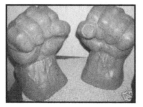

This auction is for a pair of electronic Incredible Hulk soft rubber hands that make smashing sounds when punched. In EXCELLENT used condition. Includes fresh batteries too! These are fun!!

Hi. I'm a 42-year-old Spam Editor and I'm looking to bid on your Hulk Hands, with those big, green digits. Do you think they would fit my wife, Sherl-Jean? She's a fairly full gal, maybe 220 (without her trusty poncho), but she has very narrow shoulders, more of a pear shape I suppose. She has made a Hulk costume from organic matter collected in our yard (mulch). She loves The Hulk and wants to do a fitting portrayal for this year's family Christmas card. She was mocked heavily from last year's card fiasco when her frumpy right calf muscle was exposed, so she's looking to redeem herself. If not, there's no doubt 9 cases of Twinkies will be consumed. Last year we all dressed as the Ghostbusters, posing in front of the fireplace! I was Egon. Our dog, Buster, was dressed as Casper! This year I'm portraying Captain America. In closing, could Sherl-Jean hold Buster (32 lbs.) in the upright position with the Hulk Hands on? Could the fingers grip him or would he slip away? We're dressing him as Wolverine.

Art

Depending on how you want to hold him, it may or may not work. I tried holding my Cocker with them and since there are no fingers to grip with, it doesn't really work. Now if your pooch was on a table next to you, you could probably get him on his hind legs and support him with one hand. Otherwise, Photoshopping him into the pic is always an option! JoAnne

Mouse Trap game

This auction is for the Milton Bradley game Mouse Trap. It is still in original box and is just like brand new. I don't think it was ever played with, so it is brand new condition. All the pieces are there and the board is scratch or stain free. This has always been stored in a dry smoke free environment. Thank you for looking and may God bless you.

Hello! My wife, Bonnie-Rae, and I are having mice problems with a house we recently moved in to. Our last house was haunted by the ghost of someone named Bert Lancaster (not the famous *Birdman of Alcatraz* actor). Apparently this Bert Lancaster was a mean-spirited dirty bird that was quite a successful moonshiner in the late 1800s. Anyway, Bonnie-Rae is petrified of mice and took a nasty fall after four mice ran past her bare feet while cooking last Thursday. Bruised coccyx. We tried those mice traps where you put a piece of cheese on them but they didn't work. Actually, my 7-year-old nephew, Carl-Joe, tried to eat some of that cheese right off the trap and suffered a two inch gash on his bottom lip. I decided to find some better mousetraps on eBay and found yours. I have a few questions about it. How big is the mousetrap net? Could it capture a 3-inch-long mouse? Would the ball crush the mouse or maybe just paralyze it for a bit? Is it made of steel or plastic? Thank you.

Art

Well, I am sorry to hear of your mouse troubles and I sure hope Bonnie-Rae didn't bruise too much from her nasty fall. We will pray for Carl-Joe that his lip doesn't become infected. I don't think my trap will be real effective unless you have some mice who really like to play. To answer your direct questions though: The net itself is actually plastic and the inside diameter of it is only 2 3/4 inches so a 3-inch mouse would have to pretty much be in a fetal position to get trapped. The ball is solid steel but it is only marble sized, so it might put a bruise or a small mousy goose egg on its head, but I doubt it will crush or paralyze anything bigger than a flea. I hope this helps in your decision making, you might want to consider a cat though.

FABULOUS
The Beatles
SILVER MEDALLION

This silver medallion was struck by Metalimport Ltd in 1966 and, surprisingly, despite extensive advertising, was a flop and only a very few were sold. (Possibly because at that time collections of medallions and memorabilia were not as popular as they now are.) I assume there are very few of these silver Beatles medallions about.

This wonderful commemorative silver medallion (weight 25g) has lain since 1966 in a drawer and I have just cleaned it up. It will make a marvelous, unusual and possibly valuable addition to any serious collection of Beatles memorabilia.

Hello! Go ahead and slap me, I admit to never hearing The Beatles until the year 1997. As a child prodigy in the field of archery, my childhood consisted of 14 hours of practice a day and left no room for dilly-dallying. The great archery teacher, Count Humbert II from Oxford, instructed me until I was expelled for using illegal down feathers from the Garza Chica bird (snowy egret). Naturally, I was devastated and thus have thrown myself into the world of counter-culturalism. In 1999 I toured with the singing group "The Wondering Scops," sold tie-dye shirts in Berkley in 2001, and climbed Mt. Fitzroy in Argentina with Sir P. Higginbotham in 2003. My latest adventure is collecting everything Beatles. My wife, Eunice, has granted me the wish of a Beatles memorabilia room! How would your medallion complement my Beatles salt and pepper shakers? How about my George Harrison drinking glass? Do you believe the rumor that The Beatles were to be called The June Bugs until Ringo spoke against it?

Art

Hi Art,

You have obviously led a far more colourful life than I have. While I am an admirer of the Beatles, I slightly predate them and have to confess that my admiration does not stretch to collecting their memorabilia. I acquired this medallion as I was a director of the ad agency that promoted the issue and I don't believe there are many of the medals about. Tell Eunice that this should be a rare and wonderful addition to both the drinking glasses and the salt and pepper shakers and deserves pride of place in the room. I have a feeling that The June Bugs would not have had a universal appeal—well done Ringo. Regards MIKE

Snowman Wonderland Candle Lamp

Home Interior's Handcrafted Resin & Metal Candle Lamp w/glass votive cup. 6¼" X 11". Absolutely adorable snowman holding a birdhouse cane, chatting with a friendly deer out in the winter wonderland!

Howdy there! I am attempting a stunt in which all my furniture will be fastened to the ceiling. This will include couches, armoires, tables, reclining chair, TV, etc. (ceiling fan will be attached to floor, face up). I will attempt to live this way for seven days. I am hoping to raise awareness for my favorite charity, which is to be determined at a later date. A ladder will allow me to climb into the chair or couch and sit or recline upside down. I already have straps installed to insure my safety. (TV will have cable access.) I will be allowed to sleep in a regular bed between the hours of 11:00 ᴀ.ᴍ. - and 6:00 ᴘ.ᴍ. - I need a few more items to be placed on the ceiling and believe that your Snowman Wonderland Candle Lamp would be an excellent addition and very soothing to the eye. Would it be difficult to fasten the bottom of your lamp to my stucco ceiling? Thank you for your time.

Art

WOW! Well I have got to tell you, this is certainly a "new one" for me! I don't think I, or probably anyone else for that matter, have been asked a question quite like this before!

Anyway, to answer your question, I don't think it would be difficult. The base of the lamp is resin. Depending on how you wanted it attached, I suppose. It could probably be glued on with a permanent type glue. It is not very heavy, so its weight wouldn't be an issue. I'm sure there are other more creative ways it could be attached as well. Well, whether you choose to bid on the lamp or not, let me say "Good Luck" with your stunt! Sounds like a really fun adventure! I'm sure you will probably be having some sort of media coverage for doing this? I think it's fantastic, and let me say I hope you accomplish what you want! Sandi

NWT L Ladies Sheep
Cardigan Sweater in Sage Reg. $69!!

This fun cardigan by Focus is ramie and cotton and features adorable sheep that are wearing sweaters themselves!! The little sweaters have been knit separately and then attached to the little white sheep that have black faces and feet. Too cute! The background is a subdued sage (almost looks grayish mixed with the sage) and the edges are blanket stitched in a blue-gray. Buttons are brown wood. This sweater looks great with black, jeans, or khakis! Here are the measurements:

bust: 42"
hips: 42"
length: 24"

I have been looking for a sheep sweater for my sister, Marty, and have hit pay dirt with your auction. You see, Marty's left eye was gouged out by a rabid sheep back on our farm in Kansas when she was eight years old. (The sheep's name was ironically Pokey.) Marty still wakes up screaming "No hooves! No hooves!" It's been a tough road for Marty, but she has trudged on like a champion. She was considered an outcast in our small farming town and I once had to ward off an angry mob armed with pitchforks at our door in 1983. Fast forward to 2006—she's now a professional bow hunter and I have an idea that would involve your Cardigan Sheep Sweater. She would place the sweater on a bail of hay and destroy it with poison-tipped arrows. This would give her great satisfaction and some closure as well. Along with bow hunting she's also an excellent marble player. How many inches wide are the sheep? Are their eyes red like Pokey's? How many hits before it might unravel? Thanks.

Art

Hey Art!

Ok, the little sheepies on my sweater are about 4 inches long and 2 inches high. Unfortunately for them, their eyesight is far worse than that of your sister's. You see, they have NO eyes! For purposes of satisfaction, however, you could always sew small red beads on to be the eyes! There are four sheep on the front of the sweater and one on the back. I hate to picture their cute little sweaters being poked thru, but the sweaters would provide extra cushioning to maybe make the sheep survive the onslaught longer. Can't guarantee how long the sweater would hold up. The numerous other watchers would be horrified into buying this item quickly if they knew of its possible fate!

Nancy

Chrome HANDCUFFS with Leather belt holder POLICE

We also include a real leather pouch with our highly polished, chrome handcuffs. The leather pouch has a stud to secure handcuffs tightly along with loop to thread belt through. Handcuffs come with two keys.

Please note: these handcuffs are not toys, they are real cuffs, the links between the cuffs is very strong and "welded together," the locks on the handcuffs are real! If you loose the keys you will need the fire brigade to cut you free. You will not escape or manage to force these cuffs open, you have been warned!

Hello! April 28 is our 7th annual "Dress Like William Shatner" day at our office. This is an office tradition which has become quite competitive. There are three categories to be judged on—T. J. Hooker, Captain Kirk, or wildcard, which is any random William Shatner appearance like those Priceline.com commercials or his current *Boston Legal* look. Bonus points are awarded for the most snug and life-like toupee. Last year I dressed as the classic Captain Kirk from the original *Star Trek* TV series. I talked with many dramatic pauses throughout the day. Anyway, my wife, Betty, has created a perfect replica of William Shatner's T. J. Hooker police garb complete with a badge that reads LCPD. We only need a pair of handcuffs to complete the uniform. Yours look great! Do your handcuffs match those of TV legend T. J. Hooker? I also might use them to "accidentally" lock this co-worker I don't like to his desk. How hard would it be for him to get out of them without the key? Thank you.

Art

Hello Art.

Sounds like it's going to be a lot of fun. To be honest with you I have never seen *T. J. Hooker* so I do not know what his handcuffs look like. Mine are real, not toys. If you lock somebody in them they will not escape without a hacksaw or the keys. The links are welded and are very strong. The holder is real leather with chrome stud. Why can I sell them so cheaply? I hear you cry. I import them on a large scale. Thank you for your message.

Ethnic HANDWOVEN Blanket/Throw

This is a lovely handwoven ethnic blanket or throw. I cannot tell you where it is from, but it will add a lovely ethnic touch to your décor. Feels like pure cotton or cotton/wool blend. I don't believe there is any synthetic blend in there, but fabric content is not labeled. Fringed ends. The side seams are machine finished.

Measures 50" by 80" not counting the fringe.

Condition is near excellent. There are a few small very faint yellow spots, as shown above. They should come out.

Hello and happy Chinese New Year! I work in a youth home for troubled runaway kids and luckily came across your great auction. My kids come from the hardest of backgrounds and need tons of loving care. One of our therapy techniques involves reverting back to their childhood to heal their wounds. The main one we use is called "Baby Blanket" invented by Bill Samuelian. We throw the blanket over a kid (in fetal position of course) and they shake and cry and let out their pain. My question: Do you believe that it will fit over "Jesse" who is 6'8", 310 lbs? (He actually ripped to shreds my vintage Smurfs blanket.) He has a lot of issues and needs a lot of hugs to boot. I think that he would love your Ethnic HANDWOVEN Blanket/Throw and might heal a lot quicker if covered with it. Thank you for your time.

Art

Thank you for telling me about your work. I have never heard of this therapy, but this is exactly the type of background we come from several years ago. We too ran a group home for kids with a similar background, and when I burned out from that I went back to school, got my social work degree and worked with adults with mental disorders, so my heart goes out to you and your kids. I know what difficult work you are doing and how important. I think this blanket would do very well, it is very soft. As for the size, I think it should do fine, but you would know by the measurements better than I would.

Vintage Late 60's or Early 70's Stapler Acco

THE ITEM UP FOR AUCTION IS A VINTAGE STAPLER. SAGE GREEN WITH CHROME. Good physical appearance. WORKING. SOMEONE HAS ETCHED THE INTIALS ON THE BOTTOM AND THEIR ss# ON THE SIDE. HAVE TO LOOK CLOSELY TO SEE THEM. ACCO-20 MADE IN THE USA. I did notice today 9/15/2005 that the staple plate is missing. This plate places force on the staple to fold after being stapled.

Aloha! I am a fifth grade teacher and have discovered a secret function of the stapler. While I was stapling students' homework together I noticed the sound of the extracted staple depended on the amount of force I used and the thickness of the paper. For example, when I stapled little Jimmy Moshier's homework (a very sloppy report on the economic status of South Korea and its effect on rice farms) it resonated a deep pitch. For Sally Ann Getty's report (a much shorter but well written exposé on Einstein's Theory of Relativity) the pitch was more soprano-like. Therefore, my entire class will conduct an experiment where they will perform Beethoven's Fifth Symphony using eighty-seven (87) staplers. They must figure out the correct tones, pitches and meter. They will perform it on November 1st. If not completed by that date then ALL FIELD TRIPS FOR THE REMAINDER OF THE YEAR WILL BE CANCELED! How many of these types of staplers do you have? Do you know what note it produces when pressed? High or low?

Art

WOW!!
I only have one. When I went to test the sound, depending on the surface and what was stapled, the range could be considered as high or low. I also noticed that the staple plate is missing. I did not notice this before. I will add this to my description. Because this is a vintage item, there is a squeak in the spring when pushing. I think that the tone of this item when pushed is more on the low side when doing thicker sheets. Good Luck to you and your class. Linda

3" HUGE SIMULATED DIAMOND GOLD PLATED BELLY BUTTON RINGS

CUBIC ZIRCONIAS & GOLD PLATED BELLY BUTTON RING

This belly button ring is a must-have piece to add to your collection. It has 36 very high quality simulated diamond cubic zirconias with the entire piece being 14kt gold plating.   The 7/16" barbell is 14 gauge. As you can see from the picture this one will be noticed! Retail price of over $44.95!
As always, all body jewelry is new and never worn.
From I Gotta Have It—Body Jewelry

Hello! I'm known around my circle of friends as being a crazy, fun guy. At a party it's not uncommon to see me lead the party-goers in a sing-along of Barbra Streisand's "Papa Can You Hear Me" from *Yentl* or smashing Pepsi cans on my forehead. But, due to some obsessive compulsive tendencies, I have a minor gambling problem. Last weekend I lost a bet with my friends after I told them I could eat 50 pieces of cheese toast from Sizzler. I only ate 37. My punishment for losing the bet is that I have to perform a belly dance in front of the Mayor's office. I'm looking to buy a belly button ring to complete my outfit. I already have a veil. I have an unusual problem, though. You see, I was born with what people call an "outy" belly button. It resembles a corn nut on steroids. It sticks out almost an inch. Is there any way I could fasten your belly button ring to my bulbous belly button? Would I have to pierce my "outy" first? I sometimes call him Fred. Thank you.

Art

Hi Art.

Wish I could be there to see this, sounds like fun! First, I don't know if your belly is pierced. If it is not, you would have to get it pierced, and if it is a new piercing you only can wear real gold for about the first couple of months, not gold plated or you run the chance of it getting infected, MAYBE if it is only for a couple of hours and then you sterilize your navel and don't wear it again, you might be ok. If you want to keep it pierced you would have to then return to real gold after that. I have 1 that is 316L surgical steel and is a chandelier. It dangles from above your navel. Only the ball would be on your navel and the whole belly ring dangles from above your navel so it would cover your navel, sort of. Belly dancers love this navel ring. If you don't want to get your belly pierced you can try to find a pregnancy belly ring that just snaps on and then buy a ring with dangles and try to attach it to it to look like a dancer ring but not for sure how that would look. I wish you fun on your day and I would be laughing if I saw this. Leesa

Old Buckley's Embossed Cough Syrup Bottle + Box, '40s

You are bidding on a screw cap Buckley cough syrup bottle and box, probably from the 1940s. The bottle is a nice shade of brown and is nicely embossed on the back with BUCKLEY'S in very bold letters. The box and paper label on the bottle are in good condition. The box is about 6 inches high. A nice old fashioned drugstore bottle and box for your display. Thanks for looking.

Greetings and salutations! What a find here on eBay! I have been having some odd medical conditions lately and decided to search eBay for some old school remedies. Rite Aid is of no help and employ snotty, beefy people. First my symptoms: Trouble breathing (mostly around 9:00 P.M. when reruns of *Magnum P.I.* come on TV Land), a light milky red shade around my left ear and finally when I look in the mirror I can see the silhouette of mouse ears around my right lung. I also cough up phlegm. Strange to be sure! I have tried Benadryl, Frosted Flakes and liver shots to no avail! Do you believe that your full bottle of Old Buckley's Cough Syrup can solve my condition? (My Aunt Chitter thinks I'm crazy for thinking so.) My mullet is growing! I have been diligently searching for a remedy and am thinking that Old Buckley's is the KING OF COUGH SYRUP! No one beats Old Buckley's! Will it cause warts, pimples, or my skin to crack?

Art

Hi Art, Sorry for taking so long to get back to you. I had to have a cup of coffee before I could deal with an answer. First of all, you've got to stop smoking whatever it is you are smoking, or maybe you are already overmedicated. And second, my bottle of Buckley's is not going to help you because somebody has already sucked it dry, sorry. Besides I don't think it is what you need at all. NO, what you need is Hagee's extract of cod liver oil, and, lucky for you, I happen to have a full bottle up for auction at this very moment. You still have a couple of days to get in on this rare opportunity, but don't delay. There isn't anything this elixir—and from the symptoms you described, you definitely need an elixir—won't cure. So, cut back on your medications, bid on the Hagee's oil, and forget about the Buckley's. Glen

DARK BROWN SUPER MULLET WIG
MULLET HAIR PIECE COSTUME

Brand New in package!

Our dark brown super mullet wig is one size fits all and washable.

Hello! I have written a fantastic ice-capade entitled "Mullets on Ice: Business in the Front, Party in the Back." I'm looking to buy many mullets on eBay. All types of mullets. Naturally, the play will take place on ice with skaters all donning various mullets. They will skate around doing mullet-wearing type things like watching NASCAR, throwing darts and line dancing at a bar, purchasing scratcher tickets from the local gas station, pumping quarters into a Pac-Man arcade game, etc. They will be dressed in KISS concert T-shirts. Some may wear a T-shirt with the portrait of an endangered wolf. I have one character named Marty Crantz who completes a routine by spinning (arms held high) twelve times. I am concerned that his mullet will fly off. Do you believe your mullet wig will be able to stay on Marty's head while he twirls on ice skates? Also, how flammable are your mullets? I have written a scene where a mullet's "party in the back" is caught on fire with an Olympic torch. Thank you.

Art

You would most likely need bobby pins to hold it in place because these items are not designed for ice skating. This item would most likely be very flammable as well and that could be dangerous.

FAMILY TREE WALLCHART AND INSTRUCTIONS FREE UK

OFFERED FOR SALE IS THIS NEW
FAMILY TREE WALLCHART.
IT ALSO INCLUDES INSTRUCTIONS
ON HOW TO START TRACING
YOUR FAMILY TREE.

STARTING WITH YOURSELF, YOU CAN
ADD YOUR PARENTS, GRANDPARENTS,
AND CONTINUE TO ADD YOUR
ANCESTORS.

Hello! I sort of have a twisted family tree and am in the midst of chronicling the Farkas family. We wish to document our heritage before someone else dies and we forget about them. So far we have traced my lineage all the way back to Hiram Brocca who was burned at the stake for taking part in what was documented as an improper relationship with a female fruit vendor in 1497. I suppose he could be considered the "Weird Uncle" that every family has. Anyway, in the late 1940s my grandparents, George and Martha, adopted a Sudanese boy named Dinka who later made a fortune in the glass blowing business. Apparently, Dinka made beautiful Venitian wine glasses and once sold a set to Pierre Elliott Trudeau, the controversial 15th Prime Minister of Canada. Sorry for the rambling paragraph but arc there spaces to add adopted kids like Dinka? My wife, Edith, and I look forward to completing our family tree and wish to include Dinka. We might exclude Hiram. Thanks again for your help.

Art

Hi Art.

What an interesting story. It would seem that you have a large family tree, and I am not sure that my tree chart would be suitable in that it might not have room for all of your family decedents. I am somewhat of an amateur genealogist and I have not seen a tree that allows for an adopted child to be added; normally what you do is add them as the child of the adoptive parents with a note, i.e., (Adopted), and perhaps the facts behind it. If you have a large family tree it might be as well to do it online then print it. I rather think you should add Hiram; this makes the tree more factual for future generations.

I have a worse story than that. In the 1300s one John Exley (my mothers side) accidentally killed his neigbour's son. However a feud developed between the two families and a member of the Elland family killed an aristocratic friend of John Exley by cutting his head off! As you can imagine John Exley was not too pleased about this and in retribution he and his family killed the whole of the Elland family! All of the Exley family descended from one man, John Exley.

If of interest you can go to Google and put in The Exley Elland Feud and it will come up.

Hope this is of interest and might be some help. My chart is really a starting point.

Kind Regards
Maurice

Susan Bates 6pc Set of Crochet Hooks Silvalume 3.75–6.5

Susan BATES
Silvalume
Crochet Hook Set
6pcs

Hello! The Rock Paper Scissors Northwest regionals are two months away. Last year I was ousted by Larry Cunha who caught me off guard with a Rock throw that left the crowd (and me) stunned. My prediction had Larry Cunha poised to go with Paper. I went with Scissors. In RPS, Scissors are often perceived as a clever or crafty throw, a well-planned outflanking maneuver. For the past month I've been practicing diligently in front of the mirror. It usually ends in a tie. I also stare at my wife during breakfast, rehearsing my intimidation skills. Lately, my Scissor throws have become weak. I need to strengthen my hands and fingers. This might sound odd but do you believe your crochet hooks could strengthen my hands and fingers? I figure the constant motion of my fingers crocheting would help my Scissor throw become more powerful! Do you agree? I might crochet a sheep sweater for my sister Marty. I hope to become the RPS Northwest Champion. Your crochet hooks could help me. Thank you.

Art

Hi Art,

So sorry to hear of your stoning at the RPS regionals. But it is no shame falling to the always stunning Legend Larry Cunha. Crocheting will strengthen your hands but be very careful and pace yourself. Start off with maybe a trivet and then a scarf. I wouldn't start off with a sweater—you are risking injury like knuckle strain or worse yet crochet thumb. But I do believe crochet can be very helpful for your game if done safely. I know it has helped me immensely in my Thumb Wrestling career. As a matter of fact when I practice with my self I win just over 50%, up from the low teens when I didn't crochet. So give them a try and good luck with your RPS. Hope to see you on ESPN.

In stitches,
George

HONEYSUCKLE BUTTERFLY PILLOW ~ needlepoint kit ~ FLORAL

Sweet honeysuckle surrounds one of nature's beauties in this classic needlepoint design. Perfect for finishing as a pillow or framing, the design is stitched with a combination of wool and acrylic yarn and cotton thread on a fully printed 12 mesh canvas. Pillow finishing materials are not included.

Kit contains wool and acrylic yarns, cotton thread, 12 mesh canvas printed in full color, needle and easy instructions. Canvas measures 18" x 18" (46 x 46 cm).
Finished size: 14" x 14" (36 x 36 cm)
Dimensions ~ Needlepoint ~ Kit 20021

Greetings! I have been classified as an "excessive drooler" (ED). Ever since I was a wee lad I have not been able to control my saliva. It drips, spurts, hangs like a bungee chord, and waddles down my check and chin. Childhood was not kind to me. My mother tried everything in her power to help me including fastening a home-made Drool Catcher complete with trap door for easy drainage. As a now 34 year old video game tester I have simply come to terms with my drooling issue and live one day (drip?) at a time. When testing a hot new video game I simply put a three-inch towel or a thick sponge on the floor and let the rains come down! Sometimes between games I like to take a nap and/or rest my head. I am researching pillows on eBay and was wondering how much saliva your nice pillow would be able to hold. For example, if my salivary glands produce 8 oz of saliva (spit) in an hour, would your pillow be able to soak it up? Could I wring it out or wash it by hand? Thank you.

Art

Ummm, as it is a kit and you would be providing the pillow or stuffing (or sponge) to put in it once you complete it, then the answer to your question would be totally dependent on the absorbency of the material you use. You could even put a zipper in the pillow so that you could periodically replace it with new sponge material and allow the outside to dry. I am sure hand washing would be fine.

Massive Danish Mod Design Teak Lazy Susan Centerpiece!

PLEASE FIND FOR YOUR CONSIDERATION, THIS AMAZING LAZY SUSAN IN SOLID TEAK FROM THE HOMELAND OF DANISH MOD DESIGN!

If one is designing and furnishing a space in the Danish modern motif, this would comprise the quintessential tabletop centerpiece. Would not be a stretch too far for Eames era or Atomic accessories as well.

The massive rotating tray sports no less than eight milled recesses measuring 3 ¼" in diameter and about 1/4" deep. The carousel itself is 20 ½" in diameter by 13/16" thick and is comprised of a twelve-plank lamination of solid teak! The carousel's top surface stands about 2 ¾" above table height and has a decorative milled underside edge (large cove). The stationary upper tray measures out to be 10" in dia. and adds about another one inch to the total height of the piece.

Greetings! I have an inquisitive mind that is always think-ing "out of the box." Last week, my family of eight was enjoy-ing a nice Chinese cuisine in which the food was fancily placed on a Lazy Susan. I noticed that this particular Lazy Susan had a bit of a hitch to it and was slow to spin. When I asked my third youngest daughter, Georgie, to pass the sweet n' sour sauce, it took almost seven complete seconds to reach me (a 240 degree revolution). This Susan was very lazy indeed! My mind got to thinking of how to improve this archaic and lowbrow device. Applying some slick ball bearings or possibly a tiny mo-tor, I wish to create what I would call "The Hyperactive Joe," a supped up, more efficient version of the Lazy Susan. The Cadil-lac of the kitchen table world. With your Lazy Susan, would it prove difficult to rig the bottom with nickel-based X-750 ball bearings? Is there enough space there to string along three feet worth of corrosion resistant nitronic BG-355s? Thank you.

Art

By the sounds of it, you have access to some spaceage or aircraft type hardware. I love hardware. Please tell me more about your techno knowledge regarding the bear-ings and BG-355s. I have worked with Boeing and also a helicopter plant locally in years past and have a real ap-preciation for all things mechanical and technical. Please send your e-mail address to me, and I could send some digital pictures of the undertray clearances etc. The wood base, to which the lower ball bearing race is attached, is approx. 7.5 inches in dia. Therefore the max. perimeter would be 1.83 feet. Having the bearing surface at the edge of the base would dramatically improve stability. This is a non-sedentary version of the lazy susan, and actually rotates quite well. I have lubricated the bearings with a non-gumming, ph balanced oil called camellia oil used for treating Samurai swords for millennia. I was going to reglue the top, stationary tray back into the base, but will hold off in case you are the winning bidder, so as to allow for disassembly to install better bearings. Take care and thanks for the questions. Have you considered remote control micro rocket engines at the perimeter of the rim?

VINTAGE 25" BAYONETTE DAGGER SWORD WITH SCABBARD

You are bidding on a Vintage Bayonet with Scabbard. Possibly French or Italian, this sword is an impressive 25" long, the blade alone is 20.5" in length. Blade has sharp edge and one flat edge for strength. There are some rough spots and rusting, but it is straight with no nicks. Pommel has a lot of pitting, "BF 5001" is inscribed on it. Some red paint flecks on handle and on scabbard. Scabbard is leather with metal fittings on both ends, in rough shape but consider its age. "Torino 1886" is inscribed into the leather.

Great collectible for military enthusiast.

Hello! My family has a tradition during the Christmas Holidays. After the last piece of pecan pie has been served, each family member is in charge of a skit to perform. Pressure is immense as the family has the opportunity to throw rotten fruit and vegetables at poor performances. (Let's just say last year's Mork and Mindy on Stilts ended with broccoli in my hair and avocado all over my face.) My family and I have decided to put on quite a spectacle this year. Our skit, complete with fog machine and laser lights, will be called "Chuck Childers, in the 37th Century." Naturally, I will be playing the part of Chuck Childers who was transported into the future by a science experiment gone terribly wrong. We have already secured such props as a tiki torch, 25 lbs. of bubble wrap and a water purifier. I am looking for the perfect weapon. Does your fine sword bend upon impact? How sharp are the edges and tip? Would it be safe for eight-year-old Rebekka to wield? Thank you.

Art

Hi! Wow . . . wish my family had such a great tradition. As to your question, NO! 8-year-old Rebekka should not be wielding anything like this. This item is a real bayonet, made of metal. No bending on impact, edges are sharp and tip will make a rather large hole in any family member you poke with it. Not recommended for putting on plays after pie. Have a nice day.

BULLY STICKS DOG TREATS
25 6-INCH STICKS, THICK CHEW

These Bully Sticks are the highest quality on the market. They are 100% natural and their delicious smokey flavor is guaranteed to drive your dogs wild. This product comes directly from the bull's muscle fibers and provides a fun and lasting chew. The delicious treat cleans as it satisfies. Each package contains 25 thick six-inch sticks.

Our dog, Buster, is a 165 pound Chien de Saint-Hubert (Bloodhound) who is a giant tub of energy, love, and tongue-wagging hyperactivity. Last summer we acquired Buster through a trade with a city councilman in exchange for a defaming video showing his political rival caught in an unspeakable act. But, like most dogs diagnosed with Canine ADHD, Buster cannot control his urges and destroys anything within his grasp. Taking away his squeak toy, light paddle spankings, and The Naughty Chair do not work. My wife, Corky, and I are interested in your Bully Sticks. Your description says, "This product comes directly from the bull's muscle fibers." Excellent—nothing but the best muscle fibers for Buster. Could your Bully Sticks help contain Buster's canine ADHD? Would they distract him from his hyperactive urges? Can you guarantee their effectiveness? Perhaps we could use them as a reward after his chores. (We attach a spade to his back to help cultivate our tomato crops.) Thank you.

Art

Dear Art,

Buster sounds like an extraordinary creature. He sounds like he deserves nothing but the best. The best owners, the best environment, and certainly the best treats. I can provide the treats to keep him entertained. I can guarantee he'll be more than happy. For an extra $4.95, I can randomly dip the stix in Ritalin. Just kidding. But yes, our sticks are an excellent distraction for the most hyperactive of dogs. At 165 pounds, Buster might benefit from a 12 inch Bully stick even more. Please check out the other items we currently have listed. Thanks Art!

Sincerely,

Eddie B.

SHAPEABLE RAFFIA STRAW HAT

SHAPEABLE RAFFIA STRAW HAT

You are bidding on a great new-style cowboy hat. Any one that's anyone is wearing these and so should you. It is a loose straw hat with a 4¼" Crown, and a 4" brim, that can be rolled up and shaped to your liking. These hats are extremely comfortable and come with stampede strap hatband combinations. Sizes run small, medium, large and extra large. Another great hat for the summer of fun to come!! Happy bidding!!

Howdy! I have a fabulous idea that I believe will bring happiness to many people. My brother, Ricardo, and I are looking to buy over two hundred cowboy hats. With our hats we will perch ourselves atop structures and throw the hats on people's heads as they walk by. If we land a direct hit the person gets to keep the hat FOR FREE! (Skippy Peanut Butter sponsors us.) We will throw the cowboy hats Frisbee style. It must land on their heads and rest there for five full seconds. If we misfire, then the hat is simply returned to us with no questions asked. Who wouldn't want a free cowboy hat? Especially one that is already placed on their noggin! Ricardo and I believe people will love it and also might have a good laugh. (If we make contact with someone's beverage, they will be reimbursed 50% of its original cost.) Our friend Jacque will film behind bushes and large trees. How sturdy is your fine cowboy hat? If thrown correctly, do you believe it would glide easily onto someone's head? Thank you for your time.

Art

Hello,

I can't say that I actually know the answer to this, but I will do some investigating and find out. The raffia hat, which is what you are looking at, is pretty plyable, so not sure how well it would fly. I have a western straw that is pretty firm, maybe it would land better. I'll test both and let you know.

Lori

New Jansport Buckskin Suede Vacation Fanny Waist Pack

Jansport

Brand New w/ Tag

FANNY / WAIST PACK

Made of Buckskin Suede front
with durable, water-resistant 430/430 nylon packcloth back

**Measures approx: 12" across the top
from the end of pack @ belt to the other side
plenty of room inside for** *Wallet, Keys, Snack, change purse, small camera, etc.*

Nylon waistband adjusts to MOST waist sizes
Quick release Fastex heavy-duty Buckle

Perfect for your next Vacation or Hike
*Jansport Products are made tough
and come with a* LIFETIME *warranty!*

Hello! I am set to attend the third annual Fanny Pack Lovers of America convention in Grand Forks, South Dakota, next month and I am searching eBay for some new and exciting styles of fanny packs. My local chapter of Fanny Pack Lovers, or "Pouch People" as we like to call ourselves, are all trekking together as a group. At last year's convention I entered the fashion show in the category of "most original" in which I created a fanny pack decorated with Oreos that I carved in the likeness of Regis Philbin. Much to the dismay of the audience, I lost to a fellow FPLA member who made a fanny pack out of banana leaves and Cheerios. Anyway, all my fanny packs need one of the pouches to be big enough to carry 5 pounds of beef jerky. Will any of your pouches do so? Also, could your fanny pack be fitted with Christmas lights? Thank you.

Art

Hello Art!

I can't tell you for sure whether or not 5 pounds of Beef Jerky will fit in this pack, but it's possible that it may! And I don't see why this pack could not be fitted with X-Mas lights—I would love to see some of those finished packs! I'm sorry your Regis Philbin/Oreo pack lost last year—it sounds to me like YOU should have been the winner!

Well, all I can say, is place a bid and see if you can pick up my fanny pack to try out. It's a nice roomy pack and you should be able to fit quite a bit in it.

Good luck this year—your idea is a great one!

Best wishes and I look forward to hearing back from you!

BONNIE

Vintage chrome Toastmaster toaster

Vintage toaster that STILL WORKS and is in good
condition. Chrome, measuring 8¼" long by 7" tall
and 5" wide. The toast hole openings are 5" long by
7/8" wide. The chrome is shiny, but there is some
light scratching on it, normal wear from 5 decades
of use, as I presume this Toastmaster dates from the
1950's. Has etching on the sides of 3 loops.
This was the toaster that I grew up with.

Greetings! I am CEO and president of the National Underground Toast Society (N.U.T.S.). Every year on August 15 we break from our annual meeting and sneak about town, placing toast on the evil institutions that are corrupting our country. This includes the public library, the steps of city hall, the park statue of General Custer (an avid tobacco user), and the front yard of the assistant District Attorney. We stand for freedom! We represent the downtrodden. We must be heard! We are N.U.T.S.! In 2001 we used 273 pieces of toast to spell out the words "Communist Go Home" on the front window of Starbucks with Krazy Glue. We do not agree with their use of slave harvesters in Guam. We are searching eBay for toasters so the Feds can't track and follow us in their unmarked vans. They almost got Steve last year. How many pieces of toast could your machine produce in approximately 2 hours? Could it make the 175 pieces needed to spell out "Wal-Mart is of the Devil"? Thank you.

Art

Hello Art, I am sorry but I cannot accurately calculate the number of pieces of toast that my toaster could produce per hour, as there are too many variables in the equation, ie., the darkness of the toast desired or the speed at which the toaster operator could pull the toast out of the toaster, and how hot their fingers can stand to be. I suggest you try to calculate this on a toaster you own, and estimate from there. Regards, Marcy

Thick-walled Custombilt Bent Pot—U.S. Pipe

Up for auction is a nice, lightly smoked bent pot sitter—a **Custombilt.** The nomenclature marks it as being made during the Wally Frank era (mid-70s to late 90s). This pipe is nicely carved/routed. The bowl top looks to be in very good shape and shows some really pretty grain. The walls are .5" thick (!) for a cool smoke. The vulcanite stem shows very minor teeth marks at most. The pipe is 5.75" in length, with a bowl height of almost 1.5" and a bowl width of 1.75". The pipe is in great overall shape, is light for its size, and should be a great smoker.

Hello! I come from a family of hardworking oil drillers. My grandfather, dad, and four brothers are all oil drillers. The decision to follow my dream of becoming a puppeteer and a background dancer for children's shows has resulted in me being ostracized by 83% of my family. Let's just say I hear such phrases as "Worked on any new fairy dances lately, Art?" and "Hey Art, why don't you give us a private show with your lamb puppet? Ha ha!" I wish to find some common ground with my family and figured that if I start smoking they would accept me. They are all AVID smokers and seem to enjoy how nicotine (snuff?) makes them feel. I think your fine pipe could teach me how to smoke. If I do really well on the pipe, how difficult would it be to graduate to something stronger, like good old-fashioned cigarettes? How easy is it to smoke and get a buzz off your pipe? I look forward to entering the world of smoking and your pipe could be the start of a beautiful relationship! Thank you.

Art

Hi, Art. It's hard to say about the buzz angle, because I did it in reverse—first cigarettes, and then switched to pipes. If you're not a smoker, I imagine the pipe will give you a good initiation to nicotine. The primary difference is inhaling—most cig smokers inhale and many pipe smokers don't. If you do inhale when smoking a pipe, you're liable to get a stronger jolt than from cigs due to the sheer volume of smoke one good draw on the pipe would give you. All I can tell you is that, for me, not inhaling with a good pipe and a good tobacco takes care of my craving without messing with my lungs. If you want to then graduate to cigs, it's not a hard transition. Hope my rambling helps. Good luck to your family!

Regards,
Bill

Mens Adidas Ozweeg VI Running Shoes Size 11 Like New NR

Here is a pair of ~like new~ Mens Adidas Ozweego VI running shoes, with no reserve! They were worn 1 time inside the house, they were the wrong size, but I did not have the receipt so I could not return them. They are a size 11. They are black with some white details. The tag inside reads Adidas Running Cushion. This is a great pair of athletic shoes at a very low price, they retailed for around $80.00.

Greetings! Today I watched on the television a Kenyan male win a marathon (they say it's 26.2 miles—why make them go an extra .2?). I saw him eat a banana and a slice of cheese while running! Amazing agility! I wondered aloud if he ever trained in his native land by running with cheetahs or caribous. He inspired me with his precision and determination. My wife, Janis, constantly reminds me that I'm overweight (207 lbs.), lazy, and lack simple social skills. Starting tomorrow I am setting my alarm clock for 9:30 A.M. and am going to run like the wind. I want to lose weight like those guys on that TV show. As I'm still collecting workman's comp for a "neck injury," I cannot be seen by those who might report me. Therefore, I will run across my backyard lawn 793 times a day. This should equal 1.25 miles. I found your fine running shoes on eBay. Would they have decent traction on grass? If I step in doggy doo, will it simply glide off? How about snails? Thank you.

Art

Good Morning Art, I'm so happy you found my auction and yes, they have great traction. They are doggy doo and snail resistant—what doesn't get caught in all the groves on the bottom, just slides right off, no problem. Maybe you'll want to start out walking, so you don't get anyone suspicious; they're great for walking too. If you're walking it will be much easier to eat a banana, cheese or any other snacks you might have brought with you. Well, anyway Good Luck with the weight loss. Thanks for looking at my auction. Pat

1996 Precious Moments Calendar

This 1996 wall calendar is called "Garden of Friends." This calendar is in perfect condition. Each month could be framed. There is a page that has 12 postcards still intact that could also be framed. The pictures are so colorful and cute as a button. I've had this calendar in my possession since 1996. I made a trip to the Precious Moments Chapel and purchased some items for my doll collection. I am getting ready to retire and won't have the space to keep my collection. I not only collected dolls but calendars such as this because of the beautiful pictures of the Precious Moments figures.

Hello! I love calendars! They help me rise in the morning. They make me feel very frumpy and spectacular! I had a calendar (1988) of Porsches. It's gone now, because of the goat. My Uncle Werter lays tile on Tuesdays. On Sundays I eat fried okra with mayonnaise. I attended seventy-nine band camps (triangle) in my youth. I was asked to leave because of the milk incident. NOT my fault! Starting in 1982 my mother (Edna-Marie) worked in the flute business three days a week. She made flutes from scratch. Pa loved to bowl. The calendar on the wall was OUR business. On Wednesdays Pa was home (played his harmonica till midnight). On Sundays Ma cooked her sweet potato pie. Now I collect calendars. I like ones with flowers. The ball is bouncing! I collect all types of calendars. I own over 2,300. I like the one you are selling. It looks special. Is it missing the date October 32? Has February 29 been added? I'm VERY superstitious. Is there space to add the date January 41?

Art

Hi Art: My you sound like quite a character. I THINK YOU DEFINITELY NEED TO BUY MY CALENDAR. The characters on each calendar month page would make you very happy. They are very colorful little people. The Precious Moments Dolls have very unique faces. There is a Precious Moments Chapel close to Springfield, MO, and it is spectacular. It is very heartwarming. I can't think right off who the artist is that designed the dolls. On each calendar page there is a quote. Each one is about FRIENDSHIP. April says FRIENDSHIP WILL WEATHER THE STORM. The back of the calendar says licensed by the Precious Moments Company. To answer your questions it is NO TO ALL 3. You sound like a MESS. I hope you bid on the calendar and add it to your collection.

Sharon

Women's GK Elite Leotard Gymnastics Dance Sz Medium

Up for auction is an Adult Women's GK Elite Leotard Gymnastics Dance Sz Medium. The word "Twisters" with a hurricane is embroidered on the front. It measures 14 inches from side to side (unstretched), and 25 inches from shoulder to crotch (unstretched). This leotard looks brand new, and has no snags, pulls or tears. It is a black velvet leotard. We are a smoke free household!

Greetings! After 26 years of marriage my wife, Sarah, and I are still as adventurous and crazy as the day we got married on top of Mount Vesuvius in Italy. For the past five years we managed our own little country-style restaurant called Chat N' Chew. People would come to sit and chat with friends and then chew on my world famous Hickory Slab O' Ribs or Sarah's huckleberry pie. Before that we traveled as the singing duo Scratch and Sniff. Our act was kind of like the Smothers Brothers, minus the mustache and harmonica. Sarah sniffed and I scratched. Anyway, our latest adventure is kind of nuts. We wish to be shot out of a cannon simultaneously. We are currently in negotiations with Bob Giambalvo IV of The Giambalvo Family Circus. Sarah and I are looking to purchase our cannon-shooting costumes here on eBay. Will your leotard rip or tatter when blasted forward by compressed air at 150–200 pounds per square inch? If Sarah misses the net, is there enough padding to protect her body from injury? Thank you.

Art

Art,

I think that you both sound like the greatest couple. This suit with the hurricane on the front seems like it would be perfect. I don't know if it would fall apart after being shot out of a cannon. I think she may need a little bit more padding than that. I wish you both good luck. I wish my husband and I were as adventurous as you both are.

Keitia

Women's Small Red Sequin Dress by Stenay New w/Tags

This Red Sequin Dress by Stenay is NEW WITH TAGS! Women's Size Small. Knee length, V-neck and a 6 inch slit up the back. Zips up the back with a slide hook and 2 slide hooks at the top of the teardrop opening! The shell is 100% silk, fully lined 100% Polyester. GREAT dress for that Christmas Party, Christmas get together or even New Years' Eve!

Greetings! Since my expulsion from clown school (it was planted on me), I have tried many odd jobs around town to no avail. Just yesterday after I watched the movie *Congo* I decided to return to my roots. Monkey Business. My parents were monkey trainers for 45 years and trained the famous bicycle riding, umbrella toting chimp BeBop. I chose my own path and failed (hence the clown school fiasco). I wish to now be known as Art Farkas the Magnificent. I will purchase one of my parents' monkeys (most likely Jim) and dress him up in various clothes and costumes. I will train him to play the accordion, ride a small fire engine, steal people's wallets and jump rope. We will perform on the streets together. Your auction for a lovely Red Sequin Dress looks fine and I think it would look great on Jim. Is there a zipper in the back? If so, do you think Jim could reach around and zip it himself? We will have six costumes during our act. Would Jim's 3-inch-wide arms fit through the sleeves? Thank you.

Art

Yes, there is a zipper in the back, plus a slide hook. Then a teardrop opening and 2 more slide hooks! I do not know enough about monkeys to know if he could zip it or not! His arms should fit with no problem as the arm holes are 6 1/2 inches. Thanks for asking and tons of luck with your monkey business!

Howling Wolf Tea Light Candle Holder

Chimenea-style tea light candle holder depicting a colorful picture of a howling wolf. Adorned with tassels and feathers. Representative of Native American style. Made of ceramic and measuring 11.5" tall, 5.9" diameter base, and 5.75" diameter pot. Metal stand. Holds tea lights only. Came new in box but has small white scratch on base where the opening is.

PLEASE NOTE: This is <u>not</u> Native American crafted.

Hello there and greetings! I belong to the NPAMW (National People Against Misunderstanding of Wolves) and while searching eBay for wolf items came upon your auction for a Howling Wolf Tea Light Candle Holder. As the organization's secretary I am well versed in the public's misunderstanding of this gentle and humble creature. My wife, Trudy, is currently running for the NPAMW vice-presidency against that slanderer Sid Hulme. Sid is using the "Marmalade Jelly Incident" in his campaign which is totally based on lies. Anyway, we are wondering if you had any candle holders with wolves that were not howling? We are looking to decorate our entire house with wolf memorabilia and would sure be interested if you had some non-howling wolf items. We at NPAMW have come to understand that there are more to wolves than just howling, barking, and savagely killing rabbits as some Disney movies have misled the public. They have a soft spirit when unprovoked and are very loving to their litters. Thank you.

Art

Hi—Thanks for inquiring. Unfortunately, I do not carry anything else that is wolf related. I applaud your efforts in educating the public about these magnificent creatures. I have watched many documentaries depicting the wolf as, what you have said, quite gentle creatures, family oriented and wonderful parents to their young. They just want to live in peace and harmony. I have always looked at the wolf when he howls as a majestic calling. In fact, in Native American beliefs, the wolf is one of my spirit animals. Lynn

100% Human HAIR wigs, extensions, etc. DARK BROWN

A PORTION OF ALL MY AUCTIONS GOES TO A LOCAL NO-KILL PET CHARITY. THANK YOU FOR YOUR BIDS.

O.K.—THESE THREE PACKAGES OF "HUMAN HAIR" ARE BEING SOLD "AS IS"—SINCE I KNOW NOTHING ABOUT WIGS OR HAIR EXTENSIONS. They all seem to be BRAND NEW in packages. EVE Hair Imports & Wholesale—100% Human Hair. All are dark brown.

1. **There are three "tails" of hair . . . length is approximately 15 inches. Each tail is secured with a gold band material.**
2. **This is Frenchrefined—"Wet & Wavy"—also by Eve.**
3. **The third just says from the FEMI collection.**

Greetings! I have an idea that involves your human hair extensions. The Rotary Club is holding their first wave of interviews for membership and I wish to join. But, there is a problem. The minimum age for this particular brotherhood is 45 years of age and as of now I'm sitting at 39 years. I've lied on my application, stating that I'm the ripe old age of 47 and very handy with a table saw. I have always had trouble growing facial hair and figured that a mustache would add around eight years to my appearance. This probably sounds crazy but I really want to enlist with the Rotary brass (Rotarians?) and play darts with them. Could I cut strands of your human hair extensions and paste them to my upper lip, thus creating a self-made but realistic looking mustache? How easy would it be to glue to my skin? Would it make a mustache more like Tom Selleck's or Ted Turner's? Would my mustache made from human hair droop a bit or would it stay firm? Thank you for helping me out.

Art

Dear Art—I'm sure that you could cut and paste yourself a mustache with the hair . . . but I have no idea what the finished product would look like. You could try putting it on with a substance called SPIRIT GUM—available in costume shops or probably on-line. I'd like to sell the hair extensions, so naturally I'm all for YOUR idea. However, it might be easier for you to just dye your hair or put gray streaks in it and make yourself older that way. Good luck with your membership. Elaine

Pink Depression Glass:
Small Rectangular Bowl, MINT!

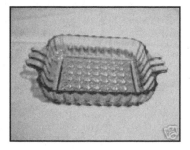

Small pink depression glass bowl, about 7 inches (including handles) by 4½ inches, with fluted design on the sides and patterned on the bottom. Bought out of a curio cabinet at an estate sale. Not marked, manufacturer unknown.

Hello and thank you! I am what some people would call an extremely upbeat and positive person. Friends and relatives have compared me to Tony Robbins on uppers. Trouble is, I can't help myself. I see the bright side of everything, am constantly encouraging others, and once saved a flock of geese by throwing my body in front of a runaway lawnmower. (I suffered minor cuts and bruises.) Last Thursday I read an article in *Gentleman's Quarterly* (GQ) that we all need to find balance in our lives. Take the good with the bad and visa versa. While doing my daily eBay searches I found your Pink Depression Glass. If I purchase and use your depressed glass, will I really become depressed? To be honest I'm a little sick and tired of being optimistic all the time. A little depression in my life might be healthy. Will your glass ware make me feel downcast, dispirited, or melancholy? If so, I might try it. Thank you for answering my questions.

Art

No no no, Art. You don't understand the nature of depression glass. The only thing depressed about it is the price! And this is not just depression glass, it's PINK depression glass. What could be less depressed than pink? Sorry, we don't think you can count on this—or the other pink depression glass pieces we have up for auction (cups and saucers)—to make you feel, as you said, "downcast, dispirited, or melancholy." If anything, it will make you feel PINK! On the other hand, if you are again attacked by the runaway lawnmower, or even worse, by those ungrateful geese (like the AFLAC commercial), having pink depression glass around should really improve your perspective. Tangentially speaking, don't believe everything you read in *Gentleman's Quarterly,* but then again, that's a whole other issue. If you want to feel "downcast, dispirited, AND melancholy," we'll be happy to write you our life stories. Thanks for finding us in your daily eBay search today!

Best, Susan & David

P.S. Who's Tony Robbins?

Briefcase Rolling - NEW - Ideal for Sales

This rolling Briefcase is in original box with tags still on. It can be carried like a normal briefcase, or when stood on end it has wheels and retractable handle. Combination locks. Would make a great case for a salesperson or any traveling businessperson who is tired of straining their arms, shoulders, back, etc.

Hello! My family is full of pranksters and are always trying to one up each other. As the youngest in the family, my brothers often ganged up on me. For example, after I picked up my date for the senior prom, Jasper and Ricky were hiding in the bushes and threw wet paint all over my rented tuxedo yelling "Remember the Alamo!" Also, this past Thanksgiving my father, Craig (retired shoe salesman), loosened the top of the salt shaker on the dinner table. Needless to say, I ended up with a mountain of unwanted salt on my piping hot mashed potatoes. Well, this Christmas is payback time for the old man! I will fill a briefcase with underwear and give it to Pops as his gift. It will be labeled BRIEF CASE. Get it? It is a case full of briefs (underwear). Some will be brand new and some won't. A hodgepodge of briefs! Do you believe your fine briefcase will be able to hold 37 pieces of underwear (Jockey, FOTL)? Could I place a pair peeking out of the side pocket? Thank you.

Art

Well sir, that is quite a lot of family history you shared. I would say 37 briefs would fit in this rolling case for sure assuming we're not talking XXXXXXL. There are pockets a-plenty for your peeking brief plan. Your father should be quite pleased to have such a nice case and 37 days' worth of drawers to boot. Who knows, he might even reenter the work force as a brief salesman.

Thanks for your interest,
Gary

Vintage General Electric GE Fan -3 Speeds - Works Great

January Vintage Fan Blowout!!! I've got four vintage fans listed this week! See them all!!

This is a great old fan. *Please note that this is for the collector only. The spaces in the cage of this fan do not meet current safety requirements and should not be used for routine household use.*

This fan has a 14" cage diameter and an overall height of 17". Wonderful Art Deco–like design to the fan blades. This worked great when I plugged it in and tested it. All three speeds worked fine and the fan rotated side to side nicely. Overall in very good condition. I have not tried to clean it up. I'll leave that to you as you restore it. A great collectible.

Greetings! Mitchell and I might buy your fan. We used to have a great working fan. I believe it was The Whopper 3000. Or maybe The Whopper Jr. 2000. (No relation to Burger King.) I'm not quite sure. My parents moved around a lot but we always took our fan with us. In fourth grade I brought it to show n' tell. Kids laughed and snickered. They mocked its fine blades and easy pull chord. It was later destroyed in the fire. Anyway, the reason why I'm telling you this is because we would dry out our deer jerky with our fan. (Maybe it was called The Double Whopper 4000. I'm not sure.) Mitchell and I recently shot ourselves a fine buck and are readying the meat. Step #4 is laying the deer meat out in a cool damp place to dry. I reminded Mitchell about our old fan and he said we need one like that. A fan that dries deer jerky is what we need. Will your fan be able to dry over 78 pounds of deer meat to make jerky? How powerful are its blades? Could we lay the pieces of meat over the fan? Thank you.

Art

Art. Sounds like you and Mitchell have quite a project going on there. I don't have any experience making deer jerky, or moose jerky, or anything like that. The closest I came was drying some tomato slices one time and I think we did that in a very slow oven. I don't find anything on this fan that suggests it might be a Whopper, but perhaps I missed it. You might be able to take some of that deer meat and grind it up into venison burger and then you could make something like a Whopper. I know that doesn't really achieve the objective, but it was just a thought that might work on one metaphysical plane or another. Now, this could be THE FAN for you and it may suit your needs just fine, but I don't want to be giving any guarantees about how it might work making deer jerky. I am concerned about whether the deer meat would keep long enough, until the auction ended and it got shipped, though, but again I don't know how the process works. The blades seem plenty strong, but you would just have to do some trial and error to see if it worked, but if it doesn't you would still have a fan that brought back some childhood memories. I hope all of this helps, good luck on the auction, and sorry about the fire.

AUSTIN AU341 MAHOGANY ACOUSTIC GUITAR PACKAGE~FREE SHIP

Austin Guitars have a long-standing reputation for great quality at prices anyone can afford. Their AU341 full size dreadnaught acoustic is an excellent value in a quality steel string intermediate guitar. The full size 341 features All Mahogany back and sides combined with a spruce top for a warm and colorful tone. The nato mahogany neck features a rosewood fretboard. The action on this guitar is factory adjusted, which means the strings will be close to the fretboard for easy playability and great intonation.

Greetings sir! First a background history: my grandparents were Hammer and Florina Farkas. I'm sure from your studies of the guitar the name Hammer Farkas is quite familiar. Despite my talented gene pool, I chose to become a hairdresser and have been shunned by my family except for sweet Cousin Maria (I do her highlights for free). When I saw your auction I became excited by the prospect of starting to play the guitar. I didn't play the guitar as a youth because I am allergic to mahogany. If I touch that cursed wood, my hands turn green, my tongue swells up and a reoccurring purple mole appears on my lower thigh. I was wondering how hard it would be to rip out the back and sides of your guitar and replace them with pine (non-allergic)? I know an Irishman named Kildoor who could do it. Thank you.

Art

Dear Art:

Very interesting story. I would definitely stay away from mahogany. About half of all acoustics are made with mahogany back and sides, but the rest should be fine. For a good beginner guitar, I would probably just recommend going with something that has a spruce top and white woods on the back and sides. We have them as low as $119.95. If you want to go a few steps up though, you can go with rosewood back and sides. Rosewood is an excellent tone wood that sounds a little more robust than mahogany. We could get you one of those for $149.95. We would love to do business with you so feel free to call us toll free at 1-866-458-8687 with any questions or to place an order and we'll be happy to help you. Thanks for your business!

Chad
www.MusiciansStorehouse.com

Exchange Select Ready-To-Use Sodium Enema Case of 24

This listing is for a case of Exchange Select Ready-To-Use Sodium Enemas

FOR RELIEF OF CONSTIPATION AND BOWEL CLEANSING
SEE PICS FOR DETAILS
THESE ARE PACKED TWO PER BOX AND THERE ARE TWELVE BOXES FOR A TOTAL OF TWENTY-FOUR USES!

Hello! Two months ago I accidentally swallowed seven 1/2-inch screws and they have caused me excruciating pain ever since. My son, Pepe, and I were working on his motorized scooter when I placed the screws in my mouth so I wouldn't drop or lose them. I was squatting, and as a vertigo sufferer I lost my balance and fell backwards with a loud thud. To my horror I had swallowed all the screws. I'm now stuck in a never-ending swirl of colon hell! I can feel those screws wreaking havoc every time I bear down "to let off some steam," so to speak. I've tried all sorts of home remedies including consuming 136 ounces of prune juice in a 12-hour period (I'll never do that again! Wowsers!). Your home enema kit is exactly what I need. Would your enema kit be able to clean out my system and help extract seven screws from my insides? They probably only weigh a few ounces. What is the maximum weight an object can be while gliding through the tubes? I guess I could try 24 times, huh? Thank you.

Art

Boy, I'm not sure on that one, these enemas are for constipation and are not the Hollywood professional ones that the stars get. It's up to you, as I am not a professional medical type person and can not advise you as to these types of phenomenon?!?

Little Tikes/Tykes Dollhouse Furniture Table & Chairs

This set includes a blue and white table, and four matching chairs. The table measures just 4 inches by 4 inches, and the chairs are only 2¾ inches high.
This furniture would be a wonderful addition to your Little Tikes Place or Grand Mansion dollhouse dining room or kitchen.
This item comes from a pet- and smoke-free home.

Hello! I am always looking at ways to upgrade my pet chinchilla's house. I love my chinchilla, Skippy, so much that I built him a little furnished casa (Mexican word for "house") next to my bed. I am quite lonely since my wife left me after finding a box of stashed Twinkies under the bed. Skippy's house consists of a small kitchen, a piece of hay for a bed, a small swing set, and electricity (he absolutely loves reruns of *Good Times).* He enjoys tiny grape nuts spread on a table for breakfast. For lunch a piece of lettuce. For dinner nacho cheese flavored corn nuts and if he's extra good then a piece of lemon meringue pie. Your Little Tikes Dollhouse Furniture would be a great addition to his house! His birthday is coming soon (Oct. 1) and I know Skippy would love a sleepover. He's struck up an unlikely relationship with a hamster named Mickey. If a leg from the table broke, would it be difficult to glue back on? They can get a little rambunctious at times. Thank you.

Art

Hi,

These are very sturdy. I've never seen one broken. The legs are really one piece with a top attached to serve as the table surface. You'd need a hammer to break a leg off. I don't see a chinchilla being able to do it. But if it does, super glue should work fine. Hope this helps.

LGA

4 wall hooks, brass-like figure: children carrying log

This is a wall hanging made out of metal (not sure what kind—possibly brass—it's fairly heavy). It depicts two children carrying a log and the third happily sitting on the log. There are four hooks at the bottom and two holes for screws. On the back it reads "Made in Italy."

The dimensions are approximately 7.5 inches long, 5 inches wide. The hooks hang approximately 1 inch from the bottom of the figure.

Hello and welcome to the theatre! I stumbled across your auction for wall hooks with children carrying a log and it caught my left eye. (I'm legally blind in my right eye due to a wild stick of bamboo.) I have a question for you concerning your eBay item. I hunt wild game and I was wondering how many pounds of dead animal your hooks could hold? I own a small, humble cabin along the Kings River and like to display my game for my visitors to see (usually my cousin Mitchell—we make deer jerky). I think your wall hooks would be perfect and add a touch of class next to my ram horns! If I stone two lynx cats (I nailed one two weeks ago hunting with large boulders and sharpened Capri-Sun straws) do you think said hooks could hold them by their feet? Maybe from their ears? How about from their floppy tails? I estimate that most of my animals on display weigh 10 lbs. each. I once hunted a wild band of sheep and made a nice winter jacket from the wool. Thank you for your time.

Art

Art,

Your question interests me, not because of its unusual nature but mainly because it deals with estimating performance of materials, and engineers such as myself love to think about such things. Unfortunately, I'm missing some critical data to make an engineering estimate of performance. The hooks did not come with their metallic composition, a specification sheet, or even a stinky MSDS. So, lacking the analytical equipment in my basement to determine the material's composition, (they make XPS equipment so big these days . . . and those NMR thingies really mess up your TV reception) and lacking access to a tensile test machine (and who wants destructive testing anyway?), I can't possibly tell you how many pounds of dead animal my hooks could hold.

Lot 36 Keys . . . Skeleton . . . Blanks & Cabinet . . . Vintage

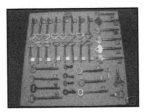

36 KEYS . . .VERY CLEAN NO RUST EXCELLENT CONDITION

Here is a nice addition to any key collection. Some skeleton, some blanks and some cabinet keys. The 3 keys in the lower right corner of photo are for a suitcase and some type of vending machine.

I don't know much about keys so if there is a collector out there that can correct any of this information, or wishes to enlighten me, please do.

Hello! I am a janitor at St. Luke's School and have fallen hard for our new cafeteria lunch lady Alice. Sometimes I stare at her from behind my wheeled trashcans, watching her mix up a giant bowl of carrot and raisin salad or fruit cocktail. Her shiny hair net, perfectly placed mole above her upper lip, and her vibrant, form-fitting kitchen apron make my heart go cuckoo. When she serves her mashed potatoes, those luscious arms are filled with so much passion. At times it's too much for me to bear. In the janitor profession we are judged by the amount and size of our keys. The bigger the key chain the more productive and important a janitor is. That's the janitor's code. We like lots of keys. I want to impress Alice with the size of my keys. First of all, would your skeleton keys fit on my 6 inch retractable key chain? Second, how heavy are they? Would they cause my belt line to droop even more? Alice doesn't need to see that I'm addicted to backside crack. Thank you.

Art

Oh, you got it bad, ain't ya? Yes, I believe the keys would fit your 6 inch rkc. They weigh 12 ounces, but if you tightened your belt another notch it might help with the crack droop. Suspenders would look even better for the total janitor package. Then you could probably go with a 12 inch rkc. If you can match the suspenders to Alice's apron, well . . . she just doesn't stand a chance! Love is in the cafeteria!! Thanks for asking.

Dept. 56 Halloween Item: Halloween Victorian House

Department 56 Halloween Victorian House

Size: 8.25 × 7.25 × 11.5", Display Anywhere, Cordless Lighting, 4 AA Batteries. This item is new and sealed in its original box. We are willing to combine shipping for multiple purchases.

After watching a fantastic episode of *Bosom Buddies* starring Tom Hanks, I have decided to find a house for my origami friends. As a laid-off Cheez Whiz salesman, I now have much time to spare. Sometimes up 'til 3:00 A.M., I create my friends with the finest construction paper. There's Gerry the milkman, Koby the local fireman, Wilbur the crafty accountant, and finally Margaret the meter maid complete with scooter. They get along so well! My next origami project is to replicate the complete bridge of the classic *Starship Enterprise* with Captain James T. Kirk and his trusty mates. I DON'T like that bald headed Jean-Luc Picard or that hideous Lieutenant Worf! I have found your Halloween House and believe it will suit my family just fine. Will my 2½-inch-tall origami family be able to fit through the doors? Wilbur is slightly taller at just over 3 inches. Is there ample room for them to stand up on the catwalk? I think they would look really cute with your Dept. 56 Halloween house.

Art

Greetings,

The doors do not open and are less than 2 inches tall as is the front porch overhang. By catwalk, I assume you are referring to the second floor balcony? It is approximately 1/2 inch wide. These buildings are attractive but they are not in proportion nor do they adhere to any scale. Finally, this is a lit, ceramic house and the light bulb generates a fair amount of heat so I would not recommend it for your paper family because I would not want Gerry, Koby, Wilbur, Margaret or Captain Kirk to be set on fire.

Thank you for your inquiry,
The HobbySuperStore Team

GOLD TRIM ITALIAN CHARM BRACELET

This auction is for a 9mm (most popular size), 18 link (medium), high quality stainless steel, gold trim, starter bracelet for Italian charms. Compatible w/all 9mm name brand charms such as Italia, UBerry, Zoppini, Nomination, etc. Personalize and customize your own bracelet by removing links and adding Italian charms, initials, birthstone, etc. For a larger size— add blank links or additional charms, for a smaller size—remove links for a custom fit.

Hello! My grandmother originated from Russia and loves how the Italians have revolutionized the bracelet world. As a child growing up in Russia, my Babushka took an early liking to jewelry. That is until her father, Igor, sold her jewels to a street vendor in a fit of drunken rage. After the Russian Gymnastics Committee deemed her too bosomy, she vowed to leave her homeland someday. She eventually married an American military man (my grandpa Harold) and came to the U.S. She now drapes herself in jewelry. Since the start of the Italian charm craze she has purchased over 1,500 charms for her assortment of bracelets. As you know Christmas is around the corner and all she wants are charms, bracelets, and more charms! My question—Do you believe that your charm bracelet could fit around her enlarged ankles (thyroid issue)? Her ankle is a size 26. She also loves to wear her vintage Prussian crown to parties and get-togethers.

Art

Hi Art,

First of all I would like to say that your grandmother sounds like a wonderful and special lady. The bracelets are approx. 7 inches long when opened end to end. I would suppose you could attach additional bracelets to make the larger size if you wanted to. I have checked with my suppliers for actual ankle bracelets for the Italian charms, but was unable to locate any that could be made larger by connecting them to others. I hope this was helpful. Thanks for inquiring.

Unisex Bijou Derby handled Cane

This is a unisex derby handle with a hardwood stained shaft with a high gloss finish with two decorative brass bands. It is 36" long with rubber tip. This is a quality product from a 107-year-old American Company. It comes in either black, burgundy, cherry or Walnut finish. Please specify which colored shaft you prefer.

Hello! I employ my own personal co-host and wish to buy him a cane for our five-year anniversary. His name is Skip Dunwoody and he's my own Ed McMahon, if you will. Skip is by my side during social activities including dining at restaurants, parties, and the gym (no shower). Skip Dunwoody laughs and utters encouraging words at everything I do. For example, at Dr. Scott Jett's Kwanzaa party I proclaimed that the good doctor exhibited poor taste in his chip selection. Skip Dunwoody responded with a hearty "Sir, you have the true gift of observation." He gave me a wink and pulled from his left pant leg a can of Original Pringles. Skip is the best! Much better than Jeffrey Sands' semi-narcoleptic co-host James T. Franklin. I thought a nice cane would serve him well since the helicopter accident left his ankle sprained. Unfortunately, Skip was born with two thumbs on his right hand (one on each side of palm). Could he grip your cane with few difficulties? Are there two grooves for his thumbs or only one? Thank you.

Art

He seems like quite a character. I have every type cane made on the market today. I only list a few for eBay. If you want an economical cane I have several—my favorite is called our soft touch which has a handle made from alien materials found in a meteorite in the State of Arizona. It comes in gray or mahogany. I can sell you one of these for the same price as the brass handled canes which are very comfortable too. I would say a two thumbed individual would enjoy either. Let me know if you would like me to send scans of any of the other canes.

Darrell

FAKE FOOD—BLACK FOREST CAKE WILL FOOL YA

This super realistic looking Black Forest Cake will look fantastic on your kitchen counter or dining room table! Cake is 5 inches in diameter and is permanently attached to a 6 inch cake round. It is topped with glistening "juicy" cherries surrounded by a row of dollops of whipped cream and frosted in dark chocolate! Item is bug proof, brand new and brought to you exclusively by Mrs. O's Kitchen, makers of fine decorative display desserts.

Greetings! Mother's 70th birthday is fast approaching (Jan. 27) and my brothers and I are planning a real wing-dinger of a party. My brothers, Larry, Carmelo, Larry Jr. and I all have issues with our mother though. Mother walked Larry Jr. to school until his junior year of high school. Carmelo was trapped in a well for 37 hours after Mother told him there was a quarter at the bottom. Larry (oldest) was forced to eat with chop sticks for an entire year after he told an Asian joke at church. And I had to rub the corns of Mother's foot every day during the summer of 1985. Mother's eyesight is deteriorating fast and she has trouble seeing what she is eating. We believe that your professionally handcrafted artificial cake would be perfect for her party. This would create the illusion that we purchased a REAL cake for her. If we placed a knife in Mother's hand, would she be able to cut through the fake cake? Could she tell the difference? Does whipped cream spoil on top of a fake cake? Thank you.

Art

Hi Art,

It's not easy to cut through one of these, although they are made of foam. She could probably tell it's not real. The black forest has a plaster of paris top so forget that one.

What I think you meant is will whipping cream on top of the cake ruin the cake? No, not really if you wash it off carefully and don't wet the cake round on the bottom. Does whipped cream spoil on top of a fake cake? It will spoil on top of anything! Go to my website and look over the selection there, then decide which one—*www.mrs-o-kitchen.com*.

Regards,
Mrs. O

Model A Ford Tool Kit Grease Gun

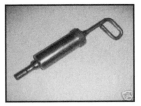

Up for auction is an Alemite lubricator for Model A Ford tool kit and also used into the mid 1930's. The grease gun has some very light pitting and is in good condition. If you have any questions please feel free to ask.

Hello! Like most good Americans I am very keen on hygiene and like to keep my body as clean and good smelling as possible. I am a huge supporter of Crest, Old Spice, and Dial soap. Lately though, I've been having difficulty with cotton swab Q-Tips as they seem to unravel and break apart quite easy inside my ear. Therefore, my ears have become clogged with nasty ear wax and I have had trouble hearing as of late. My wife, Jackie, says I need to fix my issue quickly. I placed a candle flame near my ear hoping to melt the wax, but it burned the hair off my ear lobe. I believe your grease gun is strong enough to rectify my situation. If I purchased your grease gun, could I fill it with water and shoot it directly into my ear? The flow of the water will surely extract the wax that is blocking my ear canal. Do you believe the pressure of your grease gun would be too much for my ear drums? Will the tip of the grease gun even fit inside my ear? Thank you very much and I hope to do business with you.

Art

Hello Art, the grease gun may do the trick. But please be warned it would need to be cleaned before attempting this. I am not sure if this would fit your ear canal. It seems to fit mine which I would consider to be an average size. If the tip is a little bit too big you could try a small grease fitting at the opening. You may be better off to purchase a plastic turkey baster with the rubber bulb on the end. The actual cause of your ear wax problem originates with the Q-Tips. Every time a Q-Tip is inserted into the ear a small amount of wax is compacted. One other condition that can exist is selective hearing. I suffer from this condition from time to time and have also been accused of having a blockage in my ears. The problem is that if it is something that I want to hear I can hear just fine. Hope this helps and good luck with your ear trouble. Thanks for your interest, 1low64

~Kissing Booth Halloween Costume! Nib! ~*~ Wow!~ Bin!

~*~Kissing Booth Halloween Costume! New in Box! ~*~ Wow!~*~ Buy It Now!!! Very Popular . . . Won't Last Long!

Kissing Booth Costume—Adult

How can they possibly refuse? With your irresistible good looks and that 25-cent price, you're in business! This smooching booth is sure to draw customers, even the shy ones—its red velvet curtains provide the privacy they need. And aside from its obvious perks, your kissing kiosk made of flexible foam and tubing is lightweight, so you can "work" for hours without getting tired!

One size fits most. 5'3" TO 6' TALL 105 LBS. TO 200 LBS.

I am a zoo keeper specializing in anteaters and I am excited about your kissing booth costume. You see, since Jr. High I've had no luck whatsoever with the opposite sex. When I approach women my hands shake, my pimples turn dark blue, my elbows bark, and I puff up like a blow fish. I can't even find a date at my Connect Four Club or the *Xena: Warrior Princess* conventions. How pathetic is that? Mother has said that I should be patient waiting for Mrs. Right. Mother makes the best cornbread. Well, I CAN'T FIND HER! But, with the aid of your costume my dreams may come true! I will wear your costume on the city bus, in the mall and strolling through the park with my chinchilla Skippy. People will be curious what I'm wearing. They'll say, "What's that silly lad wearing?" Beautiful women will kiss me! They just have to! Will it fit a 6 foot 7, 355 pound man even though your description says it can't? Could I bump up the price to $1.00 per kiss? Thank you.

Art

I just love your sense of humor!! You were kidding, right? Well I too hope that this kissing booth costume will draw in lots of special ladies. If nothing else you will get a lot of attention. As for the fit with your "dimensions," well, not sure on that one, the specs say it fits up to 6 ft. tall and 200 lbs. so I hope you're handy as you may have to make a few adjustments . . . side boards? I am sure your mother will be very proud of you and Skippy will enjoy the outings. What's he going to be wearing? As for changing the price, you probably won't need to as you'll be swamped with ladies all puckered up and the coins will add up fast. Especially if you run a special. Five kisses for a dollar? Times are hard and lots of ladies will be looking for a bargain, so I think you'll do well. Especially at the mall. Try the bargain basement area. Back in Junior High I knew a guy that had the same reaction to the opposite sex. Was that you? Where are you from? I hope you win the bid and wear the costume in good health. See if you can get Skippy to take pictures as I'd love to see them. Especially the ones on the city bus. Take care and have a great day!! Lyn

Very Early Toy Electric Lectric Child's Piano Works

This auction is for a very unusual early toy electric piano. It is called the "Lectric Piano." It plugs in and has an on/off switch. It is in good working order. This item measures about 16" across, 6½" deep and about 5" high. I believe the case is wood. It is covered in an ivory toned paper that can be wiped with a slightly damp sponge. There is a tiny bit of paint loss on the blue bear decal and on the drum.

Greetings! Our three-year-old daughter, Princess, has just begun piano lessons with Dr. Hans Liszt, a direct descendant of Franz Liszt the famous German composer and pianist. Despite Princess's full schedule (ballet lessons, 10-meter high dive training, spelling bee competitions) we feel the piano will be her quickest way to fame and fortune. Right now she is excelling in the three-year-old division of the NSBA and last month took the regional division by spelling "insignificant." An accomplishment to be sure, but the potential for financial gain is minimal in that business. Our family is struggling financially a bit as our investments in IOU ATM machines and Chatkins Diet Supplements (rip off) have yet to pan out. Anyway, as firm believers in animal rights we cannot condone a piano with keys made from natural ivory. We're looking for a fine, lightweight piano for easy travel. Are your piano keys made from either walrus or elephant ivory tusks? Thank you.

Art

Dear Art,

Having such a precocious 3 year old must be a huge responsibility. The stress on the whole family must be enormous. I think you should contact the Dr. Phil show. I am sure your unique situation would be fodder for at least a series of 6 of his shows. That should provide your daughter with both some exposure and some experience before a live audience. Who knows, maybe your family personalities would lend themselves to a television vérité series à la what's-his-name, the musician.

As to your question, the keys on the piano are only remotely an animal derivative. You see they are plastic which, as I'm sure you know, usually has some form of petroleum as a component. And since petroleum is (as I understand it) formed from certain organic, once live things being under immense pressure for eons, then the piano keys, while not being ivory, are to some extent animal in nature. I hope this answers your question. If there is anything further, please let me know.

Thank you,
Shanna

1952 Military Canteen w/cup and canvas holder

This is a 1952 military canteen with canvas carrier and metal cup. The canteen is metal with a chain attached to the canteen cover.

Shalom! I belong to an environmentalist group called the Tree Spirit Project, where we pose nude on huge, sinewy oak trees. We are all mesmerized by an oak's huge limbs flailing in the sky, and are moved to tears lying in the branches of this beautiful creature from the earth. (Although her moss often leaves a nasty stain on my buttocks.) Naturally, I'm a lover of trees and wish society would understand our principles of nudity with nature (we call this nudeture). Just last week my sister, Carla, called to tell me that a contractor is set to tear down our old house and build a shopping mall. This includes our childhood white oak tree (*Quercus alba*), which we both have fond memories of. Therefore, as a sign of protest I will climb our childhood tree and live within her branches in the nude. All I will take with me for survival is a water canteen and all-natural beef jerky. Do you believe your canteen will work well during my protest? Is it soft enough to also use as a pillow? Thank you.

Art

Wonderful! I hope your weather is better than ours (-4 degrees this morning)! The canteen would certainly last during your protest provided nothing unnatural happened to it. I would not care to use it for a pillow, though, since it is metal and would be hard, but it does have a canvas covering so it shouldn't freeze to your cheek! Good luck in your protest. withersfam

Nike Fleece-Lined Cap with Ear Warmers, Unisex L/XL

GENUINE NIKE BASEBALL CAP, FLEECE-LINED WITH EAR WARMERS. BLACK.
100 PERCENT POLYESTER. EAR FLAPS CAN BE WORN UP OR DOWN, JUST FOLD THEM UP. LOVELY QUALITY HAT. UNISEX L/XL.
I AM SELLING SOME SMALLER.

Greetings! As a youngster growing up in Fifty Lakes, Minnesota, I was mocked endlessly by other kids due to the size of my colossal ears. I even tried to cut off the extra cartilage with pruning shears. You see, my Dumbo-shaped lobes caused me much suffering and mental anguish. But, my luck changed in 1988 when I met model agent J. P. Williams while ringing a Salvation Army bell in front of the mall. Upon seeing my obviously exquisite hands, he offered me a contract on the spot. My hands even graced the cover of Macy's Fall 1991 catalog (showcasing a beautiful 14k gold diamond micro pave band). An unfortunate twist of fate ended my career as a giraffe from the San Diego Zoo mistook my frozen banana for barley leaves. I now work for a engineering company as a dirt tester. As it's getting quite cold outside I need a device to keep my 2 ½ by 1 ¾ inch ears warm. Do you believe your ear warmers could fit my mammoth ears? Could they keep an unusually large cochlea from frostbite?

Art

Hello Art,

Never had such a long message from anyone before. Cheered me up on this miserable damp Monday morning in the UK!! The flaps cover my ears, which measure 3 inches x 2 inches, bigger than yours. The flaps come down just under 4 inches from the edge of the cap. The other alternative I do is the Pilot/Trapper hat in fleece. These have really long flaps. Hope this all helps.

Regards,
Tony
Hats Galore

NEW! PAPER SHREDDER AUTO START/STOP WASTE BIN INCLUDED!

AUCTION DESCRIPTION: BRAND NEW! PAPER SHREDDER!
FEATURES AUTO START/STOP! WASTE BIN INCLUDED! NOT
remanufactured—BRAND NEW straight from the factory!
Identity Guard Brand Name Shredder! RAM up to 6 SHEETS IN
AT A TIME! IT'S POWERFUL ENOUGH! AUTO START—AUTO
STOP—NO SWITCHES TO WASTE YOUR TIME—JUST RAM THE
PAPER IN THERE AND IT DOES ALL THE WORK! You get the 3.8
Gallon WASTEBASKET (BIN) INCLUDED! FAST—SHREDS UP TO
12 FEET OF PAPER PER MINUTE! 8.5" wide standard letter- and
legal-sized paper can be fed right into it without folding as the
throat is 9"—it's wide enough to handle it! REVERSE switch for
clearing jams that may occur!

I'm kind of in a fix right now and may need use of a paper shredder. You see, I've been getting letters for the past seven months from this place in Washington, DC, saying that I owe them money. Something called "back taxes." They said they might take away my 1991 Chevy Lumina. I don't know why because it seems like I pay taxes all the time. When I buy a value meal at Burger King (I love those Whoppers) they always make me pay more than what the little sign says. It's like 75 cents more every time. I'm a hard worker and already have to pay child support to one lady. I don't need them taking more of my money. I figure that a paper shredder could shred those letters I get from Washington, DC, so they can't trace them. I'll just tell them I never got them. Will your paper shredder really destroy all those nasty letters to bits? Would it be impossible for those Washington, DC, guys to put together the shredded pieces of paper if they come to my house? Thank you.

Art

Art,

Well, once you buy the shredder and shred them to bits, and you put the shreds out to the trash, and it goes to the landfill, I seriously doubt they will go through a landfill just to find your shredded bits and try to put them back together one piece at a time, like a puzzle.

A safer way would be to put the bits down the toilet. Once they are wet and break apart—no one will find them, will they?

Good luck bidding and winning!

—Dave

Chessboard Game Onyx Mexican Art Imported New Handmade

Mexican Imported Onyx Chess Set

You are looking at a great Mexican imported item. This chess set comes complete with all the English chess pieces in this beautiful rose and white color. We also have more Onyx Chess sets at our *eBay Store*! All of our Onyx Chess Sets are hand-made from 100% natural onyx. Because of its natural state, colors and patterns will vary from set to set.

Bowlin's is your #1 Southwest Retailer!

- Approximately 14.5" x 14.5"
- Genuine Mexican Imported Onyx
- More Onyx Chess Sets in different sizes and colors available at our eBay store
- You can get the whole collection today

Hello! As a former Elvis impersonator I suffer from the degenerative disease Gyrosyphilities and am thus bound to my trailer. My nephew, Emerson, visits me every third Tuesday of the month. We play board games (obviously not Twister) and drink slurpees. My trailer is surrounded by curious insects which have conjured up an exciting new idea. Instead of normal chess pieces we will assign our insect friends the value of the pieces. For example, ants will represent the pawns, walking sticks will appear as bishops, moths will act as knights, june bugs will personify the rooks, butterflies will symbolize the queens, and finally large locusts will exemplify the mighty king. We will freeze-dry the insects to insure they will not hop around the board and destroy our game. Naturally, because of my medical condition I cannot leave the house to purchase a chessboard. Do you believe your excellent chessboard is big enough to hold my insects? Would a butterfly (5 cm wingspan) fit in a square? Thank you.

Art

Hello Art:

Our largest onyx chess set has squares that are 4 cm. (Therefore, your butterfly may have a tight squeeze.) May I suggest you play with a smaller LEPIDOPTERA. The larger style of our chess sets is $44.99. You can pick from colors like cream, tan, gray, rose pink, black, and dark brown. We have English or Aztec pieces. Or for other great Southwest products, you can check out our website at *BowlinOnline dot com*. Thanks again for your story which made me (and others around the office) smile! Sincerely, Robin

Halex Competition Brass Darts NIP

Up for auction is a brand new set of
Halex Competition Brass Darts. These darts
have plastic shafts, brass grips, and metronic
flights. They have never been opened.
Not sure of the weight.

Hello! I have a question about the safety of your darts. Last Christmas, Larry-Michael, Uncle Harold (disabled taffy maker), and I were having a raucous game of Blindfold Darts when disaster struck. We were playing in Grandma Gigi's garage when Larry-Michael unleashed his famous "Tony Stewart Windup" and let the dart fly. Well, let's just say we heard a blood curdling MEOW. We flicked on the lights and found Fluffy sprawled on the NASCAR garage mat with a dart stuck in her midsection. Despite our best efforts to revive Fluffy, we lost her. Later we found out from our neighbor, Jed, that you CAN give mouth-to-mouth to an animal. I wish to purchase a safer dart board and darts for Larry-Michael. He's basically been a mess since that day and I was wondering if your darts are sharp enough to penetrate the fur of an animal. For instance, if a wild dart happened to impale a small terrier (Scruffy) how much affliction would it cause? We wish to play safe darts again. Thank you.

Art

All steel-tip darts are sharp enough to penetrate the fur of an animal if thrown hard enough. If a wild dart just bounces off the dart board it probably wouldn't hurt Scruffy too bad, but if you wind up to throw a dart it will hurt any animal or human. Sorry to hear what happened to Fluffy. Have a very Merry Christmas and thanks for the question.

Estee Lauder Aramis for Men Stick Deodorant NEW

ARAMIS LIFE For MEN
by Estée Lauder
DEODORANT STICK—2.6 OZ.

ARAMIS LIFE by Aramis was launched by the designer house of Aramis in 2003. Life, it is a great game. This scent is Magnetic, Confident and Masculine. The top notes: Kumquat, Lime, Bergamont, middle notes: Cucumber, Violet Leaves, Spearmint, Cardamom, Coriander, Pepper, base notes: Olive Wood, Sandalwood, Cedarwood, Leather. Smells great!

Hello and welcome to Candyland! (I sometimes like to start out e-mails that way.) I am interested in your Estée Lauder ARAMIS for Men Stick Deodorant NEW and have a few questions and comments before I bid my hard earned money. (I design shoelaces for Nike.) You state in your well thought out item description that "This scent is Magnetic, Confident and Masculine." Well, I play basketball at the "Y" 8 times a week (twice on Fridays) and have a good friend who was wounded in the Gulf War. He now has a metal plate inserted in his middle left rib (rumors of one in his right buttock have turned up false). You state that this deodorant is "magnetic." Is this literal or metaphorically speaking? I would hate to be wearing ARAMIS while playing basketball with "Doug" and have the left side of his body cling to my armpits while shooting a lay-up. Please clarify this misunderstanding. Thank you for your time.

Art

Art, The "magnetic" is just a figure of speech—I don't think it will attract Doug in the fashion you are dreading. Should you decide to bid and win, enjoy your new scent. Thank you for your inquiry. Jackie

Ben-Gay 1934 Baume Bengue Trial size tube, box & Origin

You are bidding on a neat little item I found at a local estate sale. It is a 1934 trial size tube of Baume Bengue, commonly known as Ben-Gay, that is in its original box with leaflet enclosure telling about the origin of Baume Bengue, What It Is, etc. This is a very nice little find. The trial size tube looks to be in perfect (unused) condition. The leaflet enclosure is in good condition free from tears, wear, etc. Box shows some staining with one end flap missing, but overall is in good condition with writing and information on box clear and legible.

Welcome to my world! I am attempting a stunt to send in to Mackey's Traveling Circus. I wish to donate my services to Mackey and his fine army of comedians and freaks. I will cover myself in Icy Hot for 72 hours straight. I will start on my toes and end with my scalp as I am bald. My assistant (Jose, midget) will help me. Bathing suit will be worn. Every two hours Jose will yell, "Art, the great human fireball!" and light a match near my body. The illusion of me on fire will be evident. I will NOT be on fire! We have mirrors and a smoke machine. Flames will be two feet away from my body. People will love my act. I will balance many objects on my nose and sternum. I will ride a monkey while wearing Icy Hot lathered on my body. In February of 1994 I covered myself in mustard (Goldens) and swam the Suez Canal. Many barnacles became attached to stomach and my rinth. Would you or your family enjoy an event such as this at a circus? Also, is your Icy Hot biodegradable? It looks really nice.

Art

Yes I think my family and myself would enjoy such an event as the one you describe. Where will it take place and will videos be made for sale after the stunt? As far as my Ben Gay being biodegradable, all I can say is I'm pretty sure it is; however, the packaging and labels from the 30's do not reflect this statement anywhere, so I cannot state that it is with 100% accuracy! Debby

Lot of 12 Little Golden Books / children's books

Little Golden Books
Just in time for summer reading
This Lot Includes:
Alice in Wonderland
The Shy Little Kitten
Frosty the Snowman
Duck Tales
Prince and the Pauper
The Emperor's New Clothes
Grover Takes Care of Baby
Winnie the Pooh and the Missing Bullhorn
My First Counting Book
Talespin Ghost Ship
Tawny Scrawny Lion
Mother Goose

I'm interested in your children's books but have an interesting dilemma. My wife, Marci, and in-laws, Ray and Lynne, are driving me insane and I'm ready to light myself on fire. The first time I met my future mother-in-law she greeted me with a "So your da whittle guy dat Mawci woves so much" and pinched my cheeks. Seven years later they still talk what I call "The Devil's Language." Think of a family of overgrown Elmer Fudds. Recently, for my wife's birthday she received a locket from Ray and Lynne and screamed "My pairwents awe da best evah!" and ran into their open arms. I sat there quietly—ready to gouge my eyeballs out with my fingers. On a happier note Marci and I are expecting our first child in October and I'm purchasing some children's books. I don't want little Willy subjected to that Satanic-filled gibberish so are there any words that could be considered baby talk in your books? Words like "gwoups" or "pwincess" or "wanguage." I need to break the cycle somehow. Thank you.

Art

Art, what an interesting dilemma. I think all the books I have listed are actually in English. If you have the winning bid I can also include free of charge a set of ear plugs for you to take to family functions. Insert them in before arriving and just sit, nod and smile. If you win more than one of the lots I will combine shipping costs to make them very affordable. Thanks for the inquiry. Cheryl

Old Ceramic Bank - Retirement Fund - Comic Character

I remember these banks from the 60's, although they may have been made earlier. They all have a sign on the front of the characters (usually a Hobo lookin' fella) which reads, "Retirement Fund."

This comic little "Retirement Fund" bank is made of a very light ceramic material. His colors are still very bright with a smooth shiny surface; wear shows on the bottom & there is some grease staining on the front of the figure and on the base. He has a small chip on his right elbow & a bit of chipping from under that arm. The coin slot is on the back of the hat, and the stopper on the bottom of the bank is made of black rubber. This little guy measures about 7¼" tall & app. 4" from elbow to elbow. The base is about 3" wide.

Nice addition to your bank collection!

Great retirement gift for your favorite workin' man!

My papa is 84 years old and still works 12–14 hour days. He has worked his hands to the bone and is addicted to work. You see, mi papa Guillermo is a kumquat farmer and is known around town as Senor Kumquat or Big Papi Kumquat. He's been growing and selling those little gold gems of the citrus family for over fifty years. My brothers and sisters (Pepe, Stevie, Buddy, Alex, Hector and Marsha) have been trying to tell our papa to retire but he quickly dismisses the notion with a "No! The people must taste my kumquats! They love my kumquats! Their mouths drip with its sweet nectar!" We think your retirement fund bank might get him to think about retirement. He's an 84-year-old man with gnarly fingers that weighs 103 pounds for Pete's sake! How would it look if we covered the entire face of the grandpa with black pen? Obviously, papa Guillermo is a proud man with semi-dark skin. Also, will Mexican pesos fit in the slot? He's got about 2,000 of those. Thank you.

Art

Dear Art—

I am unsure about the size of a peso, so I measured the coin slot on the bank, which is located on the back of the hat. It is about an inch and a quarter long by about a quarter inch wide. So, it will take a pretty large coin.

As to adding color to the face, you should know that the bank is finished with a shiny glaze, so you should use a pigment which will adhere to that surface.

Thank you for the charming story about your papa, Senor Kumquat! He sounds like someone I would enjoy knowing!

Thank You for your interest—

Best Regards—

Cookie

Pink Dolomite

Dolomite, which is named for the French mineralogist Deodat de Dolomieu, is a common sedimentary rock-forming mineral that can be found in massive beds of several hundred feet thick. Dolomite in addition to the sedimentary beds is also found in metamorphic marbles, hydrothermal veins and replacement deposits. Except in its pink, curved crystal habit, dolomite is hard to distinguish from its second cousin (calcite).

Greetings! Your auction is exactly what I have been looking for! You see, the past four months a pesky crow has continued to target his business (poop) on my garden gnomes that grace my back yard. I possess an impressive collection of garden gnomes and this old crow seems to think he has free reign to vandalize them. It's time for me to be rid of this nasty delinquent once and for all. If God gave David a rock to slay Goliath with, then surely He would allow me to strike a nettlesome and provoking crow dead (or at least unconscious). I've heard that Dolomite rocks help prevent feelings of anxiety as well. Excellent. I worry about the GNP of Hungary a lot. Sometimes the number 72. I currently do not own a biblical sling like King David but possess my childhood sling shot. How far would I have to pull back on the sling shot for your rock to strike the crow down like it did Goliath? Two feet? You think the rock's too light? Would the rock's shape hinder its flight pattern in any way? Thank you.

Art

Hi. Well I must say I have never had to sort out a crow. I have been quite lucky as I have a dog and she scares away anything in our garden. The rock is heavy and it depends on how far the crow is and how good a shot you are. I am sure that if you aim, pull back, and fire you are sure to hit the pesky crow. But I can't guarantee you will hit it the first time or even hit it. But if I was the crow and you were throwing that rock at me I would be off and never return. So if you do purchase this rock, good luck and let me know how you get on.

Star Wars Lando Calrissian
12-inch Doll—MIB

You are bidding on the Lando Calrissian 12-inch Collector Series doll. This 1996 Collector's Series has never been open and has been with me for years. Though the box shows some wear, it is in great shape.

Greetings from a galaxy far, far away (Woodlake, California). I first heard about *Star Wars* early in life from Sister Judy of the Pius IV Catholic Shelter. A few years later I saw a commercial for Colt .45 malt liquor. That commercial starred Billy Dee Williams. I was crushed because BDW portrayed a prominent character in Episodes V and VI of the *Star Wars* trilogy. But I couldn't get it out of my mind that this man was trying to sell liquor to underage kids. He's Lando Calrissian for heaven's sake! Do you believe that if I were to bid on your Lando Calrissian 12-inch Doll that I would be contradicting myself? I work at a camp for recovering teenage alcoholics. I'm not sure if I could own a 12-inch doll of the spokesperson for Colt .45 malt liquor and try and help the youth of today at the same time. Additionally, do you believe Lando would have allowed alcohol on Cloud City to underaged youths? You know, he was in charge of the entire city in *The Empire Strikes Back*.

Art

Greetings fellow eBayer,

First of all, I must say I admire the fact that your question involves what may appear to be an ethical dilemma. Without the risk of being biased as the one selling the item, I see no contradiction here. If it is something you want and enjoy having, then go ahead. As far as BDW selling alcohol subliminally to underaged children, I don't see it; what I do see is a beverage company trying to capitalize on an African American movie star's (for back then) fame and market their product. Most actors/actresses, especially those up and coming, including older ones, will endorse many a product for whatever reason they decide, whether it be more fame or the ever powerful $. So, having considered what really is just probably surface reasoning and taking into consideration the fact that most of the kids you help have probably never even seen that commercial, the answer seems evidently clear.

Now as far as Lando allowing alcoholic drinks to underaged children in Cloud City, all I can tell you is that in Germany, as long as you can reach over the counter you can drink. I do not know what the age limit was long ago in that galaxy so very far away, but I'm quite sure that no matter what it is or is not, children of all ages can be pretty clever. Here in the U.S. it's 21 so drink responsibly. Hope this helps.

Tim

New in plastic 35 year anniversary Disneyland Map

New in plastic never been opened 35th anniversary souvenir pop-up map. Says on front "35 years of magic, Disneyland, souvenir pop-up map, Walt Disney's Magic Kingdom." Limited edition, not available anymore. Included is a graduation Mickey key chain.

Greetings and happy days to you and yours! I can't tell you how excited I am to have found your auction for a 35 Year Anniversary Disneyland Map. You see, I took my niece Mona and nephew Skeeter to Disneyland during the anniversary tour and tragedy struck. As we had just got our map at the Disney Gallery a frenzied Goofy (no doubt an impostor) snatched the map out of poor Mona's hand. I felt as though I was in slow motion as I went after Goofy to no avail (he gave me the slip just past Space Mountain and hid in Tom Sawyer's caves). I went to the main office to report what had happened and all they gave us were souvenir pennants and some nasty gum drops. Your item has brought me some hope and I can't wait to tell my niece and nephew about your auction. They now live on a dude ranch in Wyoming. Does your map have any gigantic creases? Are there milk, black cherry soda, or chicken nugget stains? How about other blemishes? Thank you.

Art

Hey there,

I always hope I can make someone as happy as you are. I had a friend who worked at Disneyland and acquired a few of these. I have sold two and this is my last one. I do hope Mona is happy with it. That is such a charming story and reminds me of when I was a kid and left my stuffed animal, Michael, at a Mexican restaurant. My dad rushed back to get Michael and brought him back safe and sound. He had told me that Michael was fine and he was in the back drinking margaritas. Many years later he told me he had to wrestle it out of one of the employee's hands as he was trying to take it home with him, but my dad got there in the nick of time, so I completely understand and hope this puts a smile on her face. There are no stains or creases, it has never been opened and is fully in the plastic. Maybe a little dust but I will wipe that off before I send it.

Petoskey Stone Fossil Coral Michigan Egg

Petoskey Stone Fossil Coral Michigan Paperweight Egg. App. 30 × 47 mm state stone of Michigan app. 350 million years old.

Greetings! As a devout believer in reincarnation I often find myself connected to people, animals, and other living organisms. For example, just last month my wife Yanni and I attended the local renaissance fair and I was strangely drawn to a sword swallowing court jester. After enjoying some hearty Elizabethan fare, fresh salads, and delectable Greek cuisine together I told him that I've traced myself back 65 million years ago to the Paleocene Epoch period. He was then delighted to tell me that he was once a chriacus, a raccoon-like omnivore. We laughed 'til our hearts could stand no more! I shared with him my entire reincarnation history up to inhabiting this human body (Art Farkas). I am in the midst of collecting items related to my journey and just recently purchased a 10th century Viking shield, which belonged to the body of Athils Vapnfjord. He was a lot of fun. Which ocean did your fossil egg originate from? How many total fossils can one see? Even though I was tiny, I have fond memories of the Paleocene Epoch period.

Art

WOW,
A question of which I am not sure of the answer, but I will happily pass on what I know. The North American continent actually was much further south than its present day location, maybe closer to where Florida is now and covered by a shallow sea. This shallow sea covered much of what is now the great lakes region, extending over to what is currently the state of Iowa as well. The name of this shallow sea I do not know. The number of fossils you can see is quite numerous. Each coral animal (*Hexagonaria percarinata* is its latin name, and it's app. 350 million years old and the state stone of Michigan) is about a few millimeters across, and the piece is completely covered by them so my guess would be 40–60 over the entire piece I would imagine. Hopefully that helped a little. Have a wonderful week and a great Thanksgiving!!!

Best Regards,
Sandra

MENS REFEREE JERSEY UNIFORM SHIRT LARGE

I am offering a sharp-looking Referee's short sleeve jersey. No chest pocket. Made by Majestic.

- Size is Large
- Measures 22" across the chest and 29" in length
- 100% polyester
- Made in the USA
- Excellent condition!

Hello! Due to receiving five speeding tickets in the past two months, I am imposing 20 hours of community service upon myself. I will wear a whistle and a referee shirt and call fouls on those who break real or social laws. This will help to clean up society. Waiting on street corners for someone to jay-walk, I will run up to them, blow my whistle, and yell, "Technical foul! Failure to adhere to the crosswalk." If a couple is awkwardly showing affection, I will throw a yellow flag at them and yell, "Illegal use of the hands. 15 yard penalty." I will stand by a cashier at McDonald's and blow the whistle every time they take longer than 30 seconds on a customer. Naturally, this would be a delay-of-game penalty. People need structure or there's chaos. The traffic court judge will no doubt see my good works and waive my traffic tickets. Does your referee shirt stretch easily in the sleeves and in the collar? I have a reoccurring boil on my left bicep and a one inch goiter on my neck.

Art

Thanks for your interest. The sleeves have a fair amount of stretch and the shirt has a zipper that zips down 6 inches, should be enough room for your goiter. I also have a very similar shirt in XL.

Katie

SPAD Radio Control 40 R/C Airplane ARF RC Kit Futaba JR

Whether you have been flying R/C for years or are just getting started, SPADflyer built planes are a blast to fly and are easily fixed when you have those unexpected sudden arrivals. The staff here at SPADflyer have cumulatively been flying R/C for over 40 years and have come to the conclusion that sometimes it's nice to fly something that didn't take you 100 hours to build just to find out that it's more plane than you are ready for, or you just didn't quite anticipate what would happen that day. With the SPADflyer you don't have to worry so much.

The SPADflyer is very stable in flight and can fly slow enough for the beginning gas pilot to control or fast enough to do snap rolls, outside loops or keep up in a good old-fashioned dog fight. Proportionate control surfaces allow for stable flight while giving the pilot plenty of control for a confident feeling.

Greetings! I think your SPAD radio controlled airplane would be perfect! My neighbor, Jack Whitaker, and I often play practical jokes on each other and last weekend he got me good. Real good. He knows I take great pride in my lawn, and in the middle of the night he outlined the phrase "Bird Brain" with roundup on it. Ruined my lawn? Yes. Good, clean fun? You bet. My counterattack will be tremendous. Jack Whitaker and his family (wife Eunice, kids Crosby, Juniper, and Bart) love to have a splashing good time in their spa. They whoop it up quite a bit. Using a remote controlled airplane, I will drop a mixture of sand, baking soda (Arm & Hammer), grape juice, mayonnaise, pepperoni, and pine cones right on top of their little spa party. It will be hilarious! Does your model airplane have a built-in trap door to unload my concoction? If not, I would need to create an opening in the bottom. Also, would your airplane be able to carry approximately ten pounds of the above ingredients? Thank you.

Art

Art,

I am sure you know your friend better than I do. However, you might consider the danger in what you plan. While our plane will lift a good deal, it depends on the pilot's skill. Ten pounds will be a reach and will require more than the power of a .40 engine. The bomb drop mechanism you describe has been done many times for candy drops, so the drop is not a problem if you have the skill to rig it. We don't have any planes for that sort of thing, so you will be on your own.

Happy to sell you a plane. Can't endorse the plan for bombing your neighbor.

TINY SILVER TONE SAXOPHONE LAPEL PIN BROOCH W/7 STONES

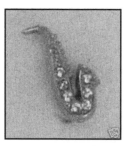

TINY SILVER TONE SAXOPHONE PIN / BROOCH WITH 7 STONES

This little pin in the shape of a saxophone measures approx. 7/16" x 15/16". It is silver tone with 7 small clear stones on the front. The pin on the back is strong. Neat gift idea for the sax player in your life.

Hello! I have been raising parrots for the past 14 years and breed them, nurture them and feed them worms. They keep me company and perform fancy tricks on tiny trampolines and chirp catchy, feel-good tunes all the day long. For Halloween last year I dressed them as the characters of the TV show *The A-Team*. Oscar got to be Mr. T. I took a picture of my *A-Team* parrots and sent it to *Ruffled Feathers* magazine for their $100 contest. I got 9th place and a $5 gift certificate for Taco Bell. November's contest at RFM is to showcase birds dressed as famous musicians. I was thinking of dressing my parrots as Kenny G. Imagine a flock of 23 birds dressed as Kenny G! What's that? It's great! I will fluff their hair and make tiny curly mullets for their heads. I need tiny saxophones for them. Will my parrots' beaks be able to fit around the mouthpiece of your tiny saxophone? How about Roger who has a beak opening of only 2 cm? How many more tiny saxophones do you have? Thank you.

Art

Good Morning Art,

Oh my goodness!! I could not imagine how you do what you do with your parrots but I'm sure I would be totally captivated when watching. Kenny G!! What a great idea. About the saxophone—if you would like, I can take another photo with a ruler or dime in the shot for something to compare the pin to. I would say the end of this sax pin is no bigger than the end of an ink pen and, as is evident in the photos, the end gradually gets a tiny bit larger than the tip of it. The whole tip of this pin measures approx. 1/8 inch long and the pin is very lightweight and would be even more light if you were to take the pin off of the backside. This is the only saxophone pin I have, sorry, wish I had more for you. Right now and until the end of the month, I am having a 50% clearance on all of my store items so the sale price of this pin is only $1.00 plus shipping.

Let me know if you would like additional photos so you may be able to better determine if Roger can hold this saxophone.

Thanks so much,
Jo

Crest SpinBrush Electric Toothbrush White/Purple NEW

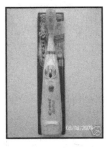

Crest SpinBrush Classic
White/Purple

Helps remove 37% more plaque than an ordinary manual brush.*

Use Crest SpinBrush™, the first battery toothbrush that combines stationary bristles with a rotating head, and you'll feel what that's like on your teeth.

Crest. See and feel the difference.

*Clinically proven.
SpinBrush™ from Crest is the first battery toothbrush with a combination of fixed and moving bristles – to give you the best of both worlds!

Who likes bad breath? How many times have you been in conversation with a person and their breath smells like a dog's? Terrible, awkward moment to be sure! I once rode a train to Tehachapi and this elderly woman (probably aged between 40–50) was talking my ear off. You guessed it, her breath stunk like Mickey Rooney's. My uncle Enoch told a story about how this kid never brushed his teeth and he grew a mole the size of a quarter on his gums! I believed that story until the age of 27. Never the less, I'm now an avid teeth brusher and consider myself somewhat compulsive. I go through approximately thirteen (13) toothbrushes a day! I once whipped out my toothbrush in the middle of a date, and needless to say she stormed out of the bowling alley. This habit is way too expensive so I switched to portable electric toothbrushes. No more midnight trips to Tito's Drugs N' Stuff! How heavy are your fabulous toothbrushes? Will they break easy in my pocket?

Art

Hi there,

Many thanks for your e-mail—I found it highly amusing—especially the bowling alley incident, albeit, all very true though!! My father is a retired dentist so obviously dental hygiene is a must in my family!! To answer your question, in my opinion these toothbrushes are highly portable and probably one of the lightest electric toothbrushes available. They weigh just over 100g but are still sturdy and of high quality as you'd expect from a leading manufacturer like Crest. I also sell the Oral B Electric Toothbrushes but these are a bit heavier, so I think the Crest one would be perfect for your needs (and I certainly don't envisage it breaking in your pocket!). The brush heads are also replaceable, so will also prove much more cost effective!!

Any other questions, please feel free to ask!!
You must have a great set of gnashers!!

Best wishes, Karen

1930's OR 40'S PRUNING SHEARS, NEW OLD STOCK

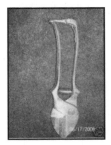

About 8½ inches overall. They make an anvil cut. They say hot drop forged steel Italy. These are a real quality tool. They came out of a long closed hardware store. These make the ones they make today look like toys.

Recently my wife's very awkward cousin, Tad Klassen, moved in with us and he's got a few issues. First of all, he's addicted to Baby Ruth candy bars and throws the wrappers wherever he wants. Second, all he does is play video games all day. And finally, he has the worst hygiene of anyone who's walked God's green Earth. He's basically a Neanderthal Man in the 21st century. My wife and I might call Oprah or Dan Rather or someone to help clean him up. Anyway, right now his toenails are so long that he is unable to wear tennis shoes, has ripped up patches of our carpet, and accidentally poked a tiny puncture wound in our cat's side as she was simply walking by. We are thinking of sneaking into his room at night and cutting (or shaving) his toenails while he sleeps. Your pruning shears might be the only instrument strong enough to break through the thick, transparent surface of his toes. Do you believe your pruning shears can cut through about 2 ½ inches worth of Tad's toenails? Thank you.

Art

Well, I thought my 85 year old father was the only one with this toenail problem. Yes they would cut through easily, however they would tend to be too big to be really effective. Use side cutters for cutting wire. They are smaller and will work better and also a Dremel grinder (rotary grinder if you have one). You can get those babies paper thin and medicine can get down and help. Use Vicks Vapo Rub rubbed in very well all over the nail and edges and underneath as much as possible. Thanks, Jim

Rare Starbucks coffee globe map travel mug with flags

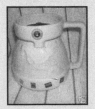

Welcome!

Up for bids is a wonderful Starbucks coffee globe/map mug.
The flags/flavor labels surround the base of the mug and in-
clude Colombia, Guatemala, Mexico, New Guinea, Sulawesi,
Sumatra, Sanani, Ethiopia Harrar, Ethiopia Yergacheffe, and
Kenya. The Starbucks logo is on both sides of the mug.
In great condition with a cap for traveling.
A great, rare mug to add to your collection!

Hello! I was talking to my neighbor last week and he said
that he knows this guy who spilled coffee on himself at a
restaurant. He sued the coffee company for millions because
the coffee was too hot! This gave me a great idea since I need
some cash. I will enter a random coffee house (NOT Starbucks
because they employ fantastic lawyers) and have their employee fill up my personal coffee cup with their house blend coffee.
When I am handed the piping hot coffee the lid will "accidentally" come off and coffee will spill all over my body. I will make
a big show, screaming, "Piping hot coffee on my body! Hot
liquids alert! Code red!" I will ask to see the manager immediately and tell him I'm suing. Then I'll hire a lawyer (hopefully
that guy that freed O.J.) and will be on the road to financial
freedom! I'm looking to buy a coffee mug here on eBay. If I
screwed open the lid, say around 2 cm, do you believe the coffee will splash out, drizzle, or explode all over me? Thank you.

Art

Hello, Art—

In reflecting on the scenario you proposed, I was struck with a question of my own. Namely, would said random coffee house actually fulfill your request to serve you in a personal cup NOT marked with the number of ounces and NOT affiliated with their own company—a worldwide competitor, nonetheless?

Regardless of the answer to that question, I am sorry to inform you that if the specifications for the particular coffee mug for which you are looking to purchase require that the lid be able to "accidentally" come off and spill coffee all over your body, this is DEFINITELY not the mug for you! It seems Starbucks has designed this mug with a very special lid and rim which provides optimal protection from spillage. It would be very difficult to "accidentally" screw open the lid ANY amount without being obvious and even if you WERE able to do so discreetly, you would need to "accidentally" tip the mug at at least a 70 degree angle in order for any liquid to even drizzle out. It would take an even greater angle to produce explosive effects and would require much jostling about to induce a splash.

In conclusion, I cannot give any guarantees as to the ability of this mug to fulfill your needs in this matter. I do require that if you purchase this mug with the intention of using it in such an endeavor, that we further discuss and contract that I will in no way be held liable for any damages or injuries resulting from the use of this mug or any mug from my auctions.

I hope this answers your question and am sorry that we will likely not be receiving your bid. Good luck in your quest for the life-altering mug, and please keep us posted should you go through with this experiment and win a lawsuit. We would like to know the type of mug best suited for this, as we could use money, too!

Prada Hydrating Face Cream for dry skin NIB Full sz

THIS AUCTION FEATURES a BRAND NEW SEALED BOX of one of the beauty industry's most wanted cult favorites to add to your skin regimen for a fraction of the original price! Take this opportunity to pamper your skin with one of the most luxurious names in skincare, or to find the perfect gift for fabulous fashion-conscious friends or relatives.

Immediately comforts dry skin with the highest quality ingredients.

FOR skin with dry tendencies.

FUNDAMENTALS:
- Hydrates dry skin and helps to support skin's optimum moisture balance.
- Glycerin shores up skin's natural ingredients.
- Aloe vera moisturizes and protects the skin.
- Allantoin soothes and stimulates skin tissue repair.
- Vitamin E protects against external damage (pollution, sun).

Hello! I have an ailment that has been diagnosed by Dr. B. D. Schultz but am looking for my own remedy. The doctor's methods are unconventional and make me uncomfortable. Nuclear shock therapy. For the twenty-second time! My issue is that I am obsessed with ordinal numbers like seventeenth and forty-second. It started in the eighth grade after bullies chased me home and threw oranges at me yelling, "Ada! Ada!" Since then, I must adhere to their will. They make me shout their names out. (One-hundred-ninety-third is why!) I scream them out at inappropriate times and am constantly counting people in line, the number of cereal boxes on a shelf, how many stop signs I've passed, etc., etc. I've been banned from buffet lines by Sizzler and Home Town Buffet (I have to be fourth in line!). I figured facial cream might cure my problem by seeping into the pores of my skin and cleansing me. Kind of like what Richard Gere does. Have you known your cream to cure any ailments? If so, do you believe it would work on mine? Could I apply it to my scalp? Thank you.

Art

Dear Art,

I was touched by your e-mail and current situation, I have a friend who is afflicted with a similar interference to her daily life. The Prada cream you inquired about is a very special blend of purifying ingredients to calm, hydrate, protect, purify, and stimulate tissue repair of the skin. The airless packaging technology Prada uses guarantees that air never mixes with the product, to insure optimum freshness and purity. However I am not sure whether or not you would want to use a lotion on your scalp, unless your head is shaven—otherwise your scalp and hair may become over moisturized. The light organic fragrance this cream diffuses personally uplifts my psyche, and calms my restless spirit, I would assume it may do the same for you—however I am not your doctor, and cannot offer you any guarantees. I hope this answers your inquiry. Happy Holidays,

Sincerely,
Liska S. K.

Warm Scented Ladybug Heating Pad/Aromatherapy/Rice pack

This "Little Lady Ladybug" is a plush heating pad. Safer than electrical heating pads for children.

When warmed in the microwave for 30 seconds up to one and a half minutes (depending on appliance) this cute ladybug comes alive with a soothing warmth and fragrance of cinnamon and cloves that is comforting to children as well as adults!!

Made of a soft flannel material, she is durable enough to withstand "Child's Play" without the problem of saturation as with similar items made of polar fleece when microwaved. She will still become damp, as this is the function of this particular "moist heat aroma therapy," and most chiropractors agree, moist heat is the best for muscle aches and pains. Her body contains rice, with bits of cinnamon and cloves so she is 100% Non-Toxic to children.

This Little Lady Ladybug is also great for tummy aches and ear aches or just a warm friend to cuddle up with.

Hello! Just last Saturday I had a terrible accident. One of our chickens got loose from its pen and found her way into our living room. As I tried to capture the obviously frightened animal she climbed the fireplace, jumped over our mounted deer hooves, and wedged herself between our Road Kill Cafe poster and our stuffed chipmunks. Rachael, my wife, was out swapping corn for cauliflower with Josiah down the road and was unavailable to assist me. As I was climbing a ladder to retrieve the chicken, it gave way, and I tumbled to the ground. My head narrowly missed our petrified dung collection but I sprained my inner thigh in the process. Preacher Eli believes I should apply ginger oil for quick healing. I thought that a simple goat's milk bath would suffice, but have seen no results. Your fabulous ladybug heating pad could speed up my recovery. How many hours do you suggest I place this ladybug heating pad on my inner thigh? Every 2 or 3 hours? Is it really for kids only?

Art

WOW, I am sorry, it sounds as if you had quite a time there. As to your question, I really cannot give medical advice. However, I was just at the chiropractor today and asked how frequently I could apply heat to my neck, and he said at least 2 times a day up to 3 times. Usually 15 to 20 minutes at a time should do the trick. This ladybug is NOT just for kids, adults love them as well!! Hope this helps. And hope you have a speedy recovery! Stephanie

Self Help Tapes
by Anthony Robbins & Denis Waitley Phd.

The Psychology of Winning
by Denis Waitley

Experience **Denis Waitley's** best-selling program **"The Psychology Of Winning."** Build self-esteem, motivation, and self-discipline while developing the 10 qualities of a total winner. You will also discover the 2 vital qualities every successful person must develop. These same qualities have helped athletes shatter world records. **Denis Waitley** reveals the same "10 Steps to Winning" taken by Olympic champions and Fortune 500 executives. Capitalize on the principles of great achievers, learn how winners continue to improve, and find out why nobody can push you as far as you push yourself.

Winning isn't just luck. You need a programmed mind set to become a champion.

You'll learn Winners' Ways to:

- Focus your dominant thoughts on leading you inevitably to victories in all your challenges
- Create a new, optimistic way of life
- Harmonize the "Three Zones of Growth" to keep yourself in the winner's circle
- Program your inner "robot" for unlimited self-discipline

In **The Psychology of Winning,** Denis explains that no race, no game is important unless you are also a winner in life. For it's only the winners in life who really enjoy the spoils of victory.

Greetings! I'm at my wit's end. I have nowhere else to turn but to your New Age auction. Ever since the "Smokey Tree Incident" my life has taken a turn for the worst. A revolving door of failed remedies has followed. I lay in front of the TV 17 hours a day eating Hot Cheetos and watching reruns of *Family Ties*. Scientology was of no help as they stole my Paxil and dumped it down the drain. I contacted a fortune teller for $50 who said I needed a face lift and to eat 10 pieces of cheese toast from Sizzler. No help indeed! Even my mom's chicken noodle soup cannot help my mental anguish. I'm willing to try anything to motivate my life! I've read that self-motivation guru Denis Watiley says that he can unlock my "inner robot for unlimited discipline." I can't wait! I didn't even know I had an inner robot! What a discovery! What a man! Have you personally listened to these tapes? Could they motivate a lonely, former pet store owner like myself? Thank you.

Art

Yes I have listened to them. They have motivated me to finish my college education and to also become a successful eBayer and now I am starting a photography studio. It all comes from within—you do have an inner robot and he will listen to what you tell him, good or bad. These tapes will help you put the good stuff inside.

Acknowledgments

Letters to eBay would never have come to life if it weren't for the following people:

My agent, Rick Broadhead, who saw from 3,000 miles away (literally) that the potential for some crazy e-mails written to eBay vendors could be turned into a book. Thank you for your support and enthusiasm that never wavered.

My editor from Warner Books, Ben Greenberg. We've sure been through a lot together—climbed Mount Kilimanjaro with little more than a tube of toothpaste and some Dennison's Chili; trekked through the swamplands of Bangladesh hunting water buffaloes; and saved those beached whales off the coast of Sri Lanka. Okay, we didn't do those things together, but you did do a fantastic job on my book.

My brothers from another mother—Dave Childers and Mike Falls, the unofficial *Letters to eBay* editors who were there from the genesis of my project. Not only that but they were there from the very beginning. Thousands of teaching hours were devoted to critiquing my letters and the world is a better place for it.

My friends and family who inspired me more than the movie *The Karate Kid* ever could have. I'm now the "Best! Around! Nothing's gonna ever keep me down." My brother-in-law Marc Welty who started it all by posting an exquisite, religious artifact on eBay. Craig and Marilyn Meadors for giving me a head start in life by sending me to preschool. Scotty Ferguson, Ray and Lynne Myers, Jeff Sands and the good people from Sands Photography, Scott Jett, Ronnie and Kelli Samuelian, Jim Moshier, The Five Scops, Gary Winter, Donny Klassen, Jeff Berger, James Berger, Craig Bowden, Chris Schultz, Team Gilmore, The Awkward Boys, Jay Pope, The Brothers Crantz, Andy and Megan Meadors, Jay and Kelly Myers, Julie Welty, Milowry, Chon Chon, Teacher Steve and the entire faculty from Traver Tech. And the ones who came before me—Lazlo Toth, Ted L. Nancy, The Wade Brothers,

Sterling Huck, Paul Davidson, and Paul Rosa. Perhaps Art Farkas can be accepted into the "Brotherhood."

And how could I ever forget the little people: Billy Barty, the guy who played Willow, and Mini-Me.

The wonderful eBay sellers who responded with heartfelt sincerity in answering the borderline absurd questions I asked about their products. Well, except for the one lady who accused me of being a stalker.

Oh, and signing those release forms helped a bit too!

And of course, my amazing, sensational, perfect little family— wife Lori and three girls, Georgie, Alex, and Ruthie. Obviously all proceeds from this book go directly into the account labeled "Future Wedding Fund."

And finally to you, the reader of this book for helping it become *The Da Vinci Code* of the humor book world. Look for *Letters to eBay: The Musical*, starring Tim Conway, Kirstie Alley, and Donald Sutherland, coming soon to a theater near you!

About the Author

Photo by Jeff Sands

ART FARKAS (aka **PAUL MEADORS**) teaches fifth grade in a California public school. He was voted class clown in high school and once received detention for making hawk calls while perched on a desk. He lives in Fresno with his wife and three daughters.